GOD CAN USE YOU!

Other titles by Clive Calver and Eric Delve

Sold Out Clive Calver
With a Church like this who needs Satan? Clive Calver
To Boldly Go Eric Delve

GOD CAN USE YOU!

CLIVE CALVER
ERIC DELVE

Marshalls

Marshalls Paperbacks
Marshall Morgan & Scott

3 Beggerwood Lane, Basingstoke, Hants, England

Copyright © Clive Calver and Eric Delve 1983
First published by Marshall Morgan & Scott 1983
Reprinted – impression number
2 3 4 5 6 – 85 84 83

All rights reserved. No part of this publication may be
reproduced, stored in a retrieval system, or transmitted,
in any form or by any means, electronic, mechanical,
photocopying, recording or otherwise, without the prior
permission of the Copyright owner.

ISBN 0 551 01010 X

Printed in Great Britain by Hunt Barnard Printing Ltd,
Aylesbury, Bucks.

Contents

Preface

On the front cover the credits for this book have been given to the two of us, but this is a team effort, and we want to say thank you to the many people who have been quietly, and (up till now) anonomously involved with us.

To Linda Graham and Brenda Day for typing the manuscript.

To Noël Halsey and Mick Payne of Cherrywood Art for the design work.

To Di Kearton for help, encouragement and proof reading.

To John Hunt for being both a great editor and a nice guy.

To Hugh Palmer for lending a little book to Eric which we have reproduced as Part 3.

To R. A. Torrey for writing it and to D. L. Moody for living it.

Most of all we need to thank our wives and children for giving us time which we could have spent with them in order to write to others.

Finally, to thank the Lord for the words and the experiences which lie behind them. We are grateful and astonished for the privilege of twelve years of preaching the gospel across the country. We will never understand, and we cannot stop being thankful, to the Living God who still chooses unlikely people!

But then . . . 'God Can Use You' – please pray that he will; that he will bless this book . . . and us.

To the glory of the King!

Clive R. Caiver, Milton Keynes
Eric Delve, Stafford
January 1983

Dedication

To Roger Forster

Who said of the authors, 'If God can use that pair he can use anybody.'

They are delighted to agree and are grateful to God who managed to use Roger Forster to reach both of them!

PART ONE

THE NEED

It is an amazing fact that the greatest need of this hour in human history is not society's need nor the Church's need but God's need. He, the all-sufficient maker of all things in all dimensions, who needs nothing, has limited himself in our planet earth. The limit he has placed upon himself is linked to the purpose for which he made our universe. He needs you.

I THE BEAUTIFUL PORTRAIT

Many Likenesses, One Picture

The Bible makes it clear that he made our universe as an environment for his greatest creation – man. Against the backdrop of the galaxies, set with mysteries such as quasars, pulsars and black holes he intended to paint a portrait of himself. A being so rich in personhood, imagination and creativity could not possibly be fully known in a single one of his creatures so he set out to make mankind. His purpose was that each man or woman would be made different from any other man or woman so that each would possess a personality unique in itself, prepared and designed from before the beginning of the universe. The whole human race was to be a definitive, living portrait of the living God set against the canvas of creation. So he, the only God, spoke from the mystery of his threefold personality and said: 'Let us make man in our image.' To be human is to have a marvellous privilege. Each of us is an expression of the creative imagination of the living God and because he never repeats himself, the opportunity he, the artist, has to express himself in 'me', his masterpiece, will never occur in the same way again.

Now it must be clear to anyone that something has gone wrong with mankind – men and women consistently fail to demonstrate Godlikeness. Selfishness and greed rape the earth's resources, cruelty and lust pervert individual relationships and in the political realm man's corruption shows in the way the great principles of democracy are degraded. The nobility of the Gettysburg address: 'government of the people, for the people, by the people' has been reduced to the cynical bribery of the consumer society, 'give them what they want.' While on the totalitarian side the great visions of so-called revolutionary movements, both marxist and fascist, have been betrayed repeatedly in bloody repression and the greedy élitism of opportunists in the new ruling classes.

Freedom to Rebel

The reason for this obvious failure is simple. It takes God to be a man. God made us in his image, equipping each of us uniquely to demonstrate him to the watching world and to the unnumbered population of the heavenly dimension. But the nature of God is not determined by any outside force. Moses had the nerve to ask God for his name. God's answer was, in effect, 'Moses, I don't need a name. Please don't confuse me with other "gods". "I am what I am" – better translated "I am becoming what I am becoming".' So the one and only God, revealed to Abraham and the Israelis and later made flesh in Jesus Christ is, all he is, *because he wants to be*. He is holy, loving, fair and good for no reason but this, *he chooses to be so*.

So making man and woman in his own image did not mean just giving each emotions, intellect, creative power, etc. but, above all, the power to choose. Why is this so important? Because God is alone, the only one there is. The threefold God of the Bible declares: 'I am the Lord; that is my name! I will not give my glory to another.' None else is like him and no one can ever develop themselves to become like him. We cannot evolve to God-likeness. So when God made man in his own image, he gave him all he needed to be a glorious portrait of the creator except for one missing factor – himself. For only God is like God! So in order to fulfil the purpose for which he was made, to be like God – man must have what God alone can give – the God-likeness of God himself. Nothing else will do. That is why God gave us the ability to choose – so that just as God chooses to be who he is, we might choose his purpose for our lives and receive him.

God made each of us as a dwelling-place for himself and we make no sense until he lives at the centre of our beings. But he will not come in until we invite him to do so. All that has gone wrong with our world can be traced back to the decision 'Adam' (man) made *not* to receive the life offered by God, opting instead to occupy the 'God spot' in his human nature himself.

It takes God to be a man – as God intended man to be – and modern man demonstrates over and over again that he has not got what it takes. The beautiful portrait – the image of God – has been slashed repeatedly, muddied, defiled, vandalised. Only God can restore it.

But the purpose of God was not just that man

should be the unfolding revelation of God's nature. He had and still has a further purpose in mind – that man should reign over creation in partnership with his creator. The first inkling of this fantastic idea is in the instructions given to the first humans. (Remember, the Bible definition of human is 'made in the image of God' and having a capacity for conscious relationship with the creator unique to created things.) In this short passage, Genesis 1:28, the maker and owner of all things delegates to man his own authority over the earth and the animal kingdom. It is the beginning of a process in which God will progressively unveil his destiny for man, finishing with the promise of Jesus: 'He who conquers, I will grant him to sit with me on my throne,' and the declaration: 'They shall reign for ever and ever.'

The Blighted Earth

Why did God require such a being? The Bible gives only hints as to the reasons – one such hint occurs in Psalm 8 where David says, as he thinks of the creation of man, 'thou hast founded a bulwark because of thy foes, to still the enemy and the avenger.' It seems clear that the great archangel Lucifer had rebelled to become Satan long before the creation of the human race. It also seems clear that he had some relationship to the earth. Some have suggested that it was Satan who made the earth 'formless and empty' (Gen. 1:2 NIV) blighting God's creation. Whether or not this is true we know that God delegated his earthly authority to man and deliberately allowed man to face temptation from Satan. The temptation was that men should do as Satan had done – take God-given authority and use it to rebel against the God who gave it. Stupid? Of course. But it was put rather cleverly.

The Infection of Doubt

Did God really say . . .? The beginning of Satan's strategy is to infect the creature with doubt, firstly about whether or not God has truly spoken. Nobody living in our world can be unaware that the tactic is unchanged today. Attacks on the Bible and the whole structure of Christian doctrine have left many ordinary Christians unsure of what they believe and have strengthened the cynicism of those outside the faith. The second part of the infection is doubt about the aims of the creator. God prohibited the fruit of one tree. The question 'Did God really say, "You must not eat from any tree in the garden"?' was calculated to leave behind an impression of a miserable, joyless God whose only desire was to deny his creatures pleasure and fulfilment. This is still one of his tactics today. And sometimes we Christians act and speak so that we leave people thinking that our God's only joy is to find an occupation that gives pleasure to people and then prohibit them from doing it!

The Barefaced Lie

You will not surely die . . . Even when someone is aware of the nature of God, so that they can deny the charge that he is a misery and show that his warnings of disaster are reasonable, Satan does not give up. He denies flatly that sin really has the consequences God says. We have all done it and heard others do it. 'A little bit of adultery is quite good for a marriage really.' 'People who work here are entitled to stationery/ car park, etc., it doesn't do any harm.' And in the widespread belief that, 'There is a little bit of God in everybody,' he proclaims that sin has not brought spiritual death at all. The huge numbers of people, even in the materialistic West, who believe in reincarnation are another facet of that denial, 'You will not surely die.' Satan emphatically believes in the value of a big, confident lie.

The Cynical Poison
God knows that when you eat . . . Here is the real poison. After doubt and denial comes a direct attack on the character of God. Satan says, 'The reason that God denies you this thing is simply that he is full of pride and envy and he is afraid of you. So he wants to keep you from this because it will give you power and wisdom equal to his own.' That terrible slur on the Father's character has left a deep scar in every man and woman. The greatest difficulty human beings have, even in church circles, is the feeling that God must have some selfish end in view. Our biggest problem is truly believing that God loves 'me' simply because he *is* love and can only treat me *in* love.

The Deception Continues
I have tried to show that Satan's tactics as recorded in the third chapter of Genesis have not changed at all. He continues to deceive men and women as he always did and so reduces them to the level of his slaves, even when they do not know he exists. The honesty and love basic to God's character prevent him from settling issues of this kind by the use of superior force. He cannot and will not bully his way into the heart or mind of man, nor will he answer Hell's accusation simply by crushing Satan. That would be to adopt the tactics of the enemy – if God were to act in such a way, then he himself would fall and the whole universe become a colony of Hell. Satan's rebellion is the rebellion of creature against creator, and if God is to remain just and fair, it must be answered by another creature.

And that is the God-appointed role of man. If God is to give the lie to the outrageous accusations made against him, he needs people who will give themselves to him completely. As they surrender themselves to his presence, he will fill them with his character and demonstrate what he is really like. As they commit themselves to his purpose he will give them his kingdom authority and they will finish the conquest of the one who made the accusations – Satan.

It must be obvious that such a programme calls for a quality of commitment from ordinary Christian people that is unusual in most of our churches in the Western world. So do we need yet another call to commitment? The answer to that must be, NO! – not if our further commitment is just a new version of last year's model.

II DAWN BREAKS – DARKNESS FLEES

The Trade-In Christian

Our consumer society, with its fundamental principle of built-in obsolescence, has encouraged the growth of the throw-away mentality. And this attitude has sunk deep into us, affecting our behaviour in our spiritual lives as in everything else. So year after year good sincere Christians trade in last year's experience for this year's sensation. Some have gone through a succession of conversion, commitment, repentance, consecration, recommitment, renewal, infilling with the Spirit, more consecration, etc., until their brains are almost totally scrambled, their psychologies wobbling from one extreme to the other, and their spirits desolated by alternating waves of blessing and disappointment. This may be an extreme description – a caricature – but there is enough of a likeness there for me to recognise myself.

And why is this insane parade necessary? Is Christianity a fraud? Does it, simply, not work? These are not necessarily the right questions. If we saw a man take delivery of a new car, run it for a few weeks until something went wrong, or until it ran out of fuel, and then return for a different model on the grounds that the previous one was 'no good', we would have to say, 'There is not much wrong with that man's car but there is a lot wrong with the way he relates to it.' In other words we would query his understanding of the motor car, not the principle of internal combustion. The man who does not regularly fill the fuel tank will soon run out. The woman who ignores the maker's instructions and never services her car eventually faces complete breakdown. And the man, so thrilled with his car that he sits in his garage all day, revving the engine just for the excitement, will inevitably blow it up. None of them will get very far.

There is *power* in Christianity, not simply the intellectual power of its doctrines, the moral power of its ethics, or the philosophical power of its ideas, but ultimate, limitless power – the power of the living God himself.

Enter the Demon King

Then why do so few Christians show the vital signs that would indicate to others the power and presence of God? Ultimately the answer to that question lies in the activity of Satan. Examining his tactics is always boring – C. S. Lewis once likened it to chewing sand. The notion that the Prince of Darkness is exciting is an illusion cherished only by those who have never faced him in battle. Satan's plans are about as exciting as watching paint dry. In fact, paint drying is a far more attractive spectacle.

There are those, of course, who do not believe that any prince of evil even exists, just a principle of wickedness vaguely floating around. That is a view as wholly unrealistic as that of the people who deny that

Hitler had anything to do with Nazism! The ingenuity of evil worldwide points to a guiding intelligence beyond man. The subtlety of global institutional evil points to a plan with long-term aims way beyond the short-lived dreams of men. The strategy of evil in space and time indicates a sustaining will behind it all.

The evidence accumulates to show the reality of a presiding genius whom the Bible calls by many names: among them the Devil – accuser, inventor of lying slanders; Beelzebub – Lord of the flies, master of corruption; Belial – lawless, worthless, reckless; Abaddan (Heb), Apollyon (Gk) – the destroyer; Satan – hateful accuser. As an angel he was and is a created being. Created good and styled (in a prophecy against the king of Babylon) Lucifer – 'morning star, son of the dawn' (Isa. 14:12) – he was apparently one of the most beautiful angels of heaven, some have even said the most beautiful of all. Clearly heavenly light streamed from him – interestingly, the Bible says he retains the ability to disguise himself as an 'angel of light' (2 Cor. 11:14). In his power and glory he apparently became proud and tried to take God's throne. Those angels who sided with him in rebellion against God became like him – demons. So he is called prince of demons. It is this malicious, hateful, shallow, destructive person who opposes God's purpose here on earth, dogging every step of the Christian.

Now many Christians fall into Satan's own trap by developing an unhealthy obsession with him, so that to them he seems almost the equal of God, evil and opposite. Indeed, in the writings and speech of some it is hard to avoid a distinct impression of Dualism. But the Devil is not the equal of God – he has none of the attributes of God: his knowledge, though great, is limited, his power always limited is diminished and lessening, his presence is felt in only a small part of creation. These things sometimes seem to us to be infinite because here in planet earth his authority has been localised by the fall of mankind.

When man (Adam) and woman (Eve) obeyed Satan in the garden, he became their prince or ruler. And since their yielding was a spiritual act involving the rejection of God as their ruler and life force, Satan also became their God. Now we have already seen that God had delivered authority over the earth and its resources to man. In the moment of rebellion against God and allegiance to Satan, all that man ruled over passed with him under the authority of the enemy. So Satan became 'prince/ruler of this world', a title whose truth is established by Jesus' using it on three occasions, and 'God of this world' (better, 'God of this age'). When it is realised that the earth under our feet has never passed from God's ownership – 'The earth is the Lord's' – and that the present age is scheduled to finish in the hands of the one who began it – 'I am Alpha and Omega, the beginning and the ending, saith the Lord' (Rev. 1:8 AV) – then the limitation on Satan can be clearly seen. His only chance to translate his localised, temporary 'divinity' and lordship into universal, eternal kingdom came when Jesus walked the earth.

Veiled in flesh the Godhead see
The astounding thing is that even in a fallen world where men lived, confused by the swirling eddies of competing philosophies and ideas, and evil seemed triumphant, God found a man – Abraham. From him there grew a family, a nation, an empire, then came collapse, exile and despair, but through it all a small number were faithful to God. And in the steady un-

veiling of his purpose they received their own eternal significance.

Eventually, one night in a star-burst of angels, God announced that at last a man was born, who was man as he, the creator, intended man the creature to be. Jesus the man was amazing because he *was* man, fulfilling the original purpose – he was the image of God. The eternal Son of God, through whom creation happened, had entered his own creation as a creature. God became man. Then began the most protracted siege of one man's integrity, sexual purity and self-lessness that history has ever known. Satan tried day after day to find the key by which he could enter Jesus and make him his slave. Since Jesus was God in flesh, the whole universe hung in the balance, but Jesus the man, the second Adam, was committed in love to his Father, to his Father's word and his Father's Kingdom.

By the time he lived, that first Adam's choice rein-forced millions of times by the compounded wicked-ness of men hung in the air like something tangible. So the attack he sustained was similar in kind to that endured by the first Adam but many times greater in power. We will never know what it meant to him to endure the pressure of evil all around and the con-stantly renewed attentions of Hell's demons. He did it gladly. He never complained. In fact, far from being overwhelmed he began to permeate the world around him with heavenly life.

The Reliable Revelation
Most of Jesus' temptations are not known to us but the end of the great forty-day confrontation in the wilderness makes it clear that one of the secrets of his power as a man was his total confidence in the objec-tive truth of the Jewish Bible, which we now call the

Old Testament. By the time of Jesus there were already teachers who were asking, did the text 'really mean' what it said. And the highly relativistic outlook of Greek philosophy dominated the whole known world. Most educated men believed that there were many ways to God, or the gods, and that all were equally good or bad. Into this scene Jesus came, demonstrating total conviction that there was a living God who had spoken to men and his revelation was infallible.

The Fantastic Father

Jesus exhibited no doubts at all about the character of that God. As far as he was concerned God was utterly good, loving and fair. In fact many of Jesus' parables were directed to bringing that home to people. The character of his Father formed a major part of his teaching, not just because he thought it was a good idea but because it was the foundation of his life. His whole life was a relationship of total giving to and receiving from the Father God. So he was a real man, and only a man, with this difference; in him was the hidden factor that made him different from all other men – God himself. This was not because Jesus was God but because he was man, man as he, the creator had intended man to be – a dwelling-place for God. So as he proclaimed to men the fulfilment of creation's purpose and the completion of the long history of mankind in the coming kingdom of God, he bubbled with gladness. Joy streamed out of him like a river. He *knew* the God of whom he preached and knew that his nature was love and his presence *joy*.

The Satanic strategy failed with Jesus because Jesus was a man of conviction. He was certain of the truth of the written word of God. Confronted by doubts about the aims of the creator, and his purposes for men and women, he gave himself again in love to his Father and knew that God wishes all men and all women always joy.

Face to Face

When the woman of Samaria met Jesus at the well his glorious certainty swallowed up her torment of doubt, guilt and insecurity and gave her what he promised, 'a spring of water welling up to eternal life.' The same Father had come to her.

On another occasion the heat of the afternoon sun was relieved by a breeze from the sea as hundreds crammed into and around the little house where Jesus sat teaching. Representatives from synagogues all over Galilee, distant parts of Judaea and even from the capital city of Jerusalem had come to hear him. Suddenly there was a rustling on the roof and a flake of plaster floated on to a learned pate. Someone was coming through the roof! Unable to reach Jesus by any other route the four friends of the paralysed man tore the tiles away and lowered their friend to the ground. Jesus looked at him and saw the chains of guilt that paralysed him and the confession of failure in his eyes. 'Friend,' he said, 'your sins are forgiven.'

And there was that smart dinner party, where leading citizens, business men, university lecturers, teachers and clergy sat, cosy in their superiority. They had all contrived to arrive early so that only Jesus sat at the table with feet unwashed and hair still windswept, dusty from the road. Then in she came, the local prostitute, complete with handbag slung over her shoulder. What secrets she might have known about that respectable group! But she ignored them, went straight to Jesus and wept, her tears falling on his feet (he was reclining at table on a small couch) and then she took her loose hanging hair and wiped her tears and the dust of the road from his feet. In horror, the host, the senior clergyman present, watched and judged in his heart. The story Jesus then told was pointed sharply against him and his self-righteous friends, but the best words came at the end, 'I tell you, her many sins have been forgiven . . .' The glorious relief of hearing such words about my sin! Jesus could pronounce forgiveness with full authority not just because he knew he was the God-sent sacrifice for sin but because he knew his Father's heart.

The Power of Darkness

Think for a moment of all we know of Jesus – the earthy wisdom of his teaching, the unprecedented privacy of his miracles, his wit and humour, the twinkle in his eyes, the tears, the pain and the heart-break. He was a man. And the impact he made was due entirely to the fact that he, a man, lived each moment as God intended him to live it. He had nothing more going for him than you or I. It is simply that he was totally available to the Father and so the Father was totally available to him. And that is what it means to be human.

All through the time of Jesus' ministry his path was touched by the darkening shadow of the cross. Again and again he referred to it, warning his disciples of the pain and disgrace to come. But by the time it came, and he staggered through the city battered, bleeding, covered in spit, they had heard nothing of his warnings. With the selective attention of those who do not want to hear they had deafened themselves to his pain. It seems obvious that at that moment his greatest anguish was the awful dark loneliness. He bore it all alone.

Satan's opportunity was never greater. But even

here Jesus' relationship with his Father sustained him just as it condemned him. After all, that was the crunch question: 'Are you the Son of God, then?' Even now he could deny it and live. Even now he could take the forbidden fruit, seize control over his own life, exclude his Father and live – a dead man like the rest of us. Thank God he did not. Standing before the assembled power of Church and State he affirmed what he knew to be the truth about himself, his God and Father: 'I am; and you will see the Son of man seated at the right hand of power, and coming with the clouds of heaven.' What a man! No wonder the world's greatest composers have returned to this scene again and again, trying to compose music worthy of it. Here is the heart of the human story. Here is what it means to be a man or woman: to know God's purpose and to commit oneself to it no matter what it may cost. By the end of that day Jesus was dead and his followers were scattered. He had lived his whole life and died, not on the basis that he was Son of God and therefore could cope with the pressures and the pain; such an attitude would have denied his manhood. Instead he had lived all through as a human being totally dependent on the God who made him. For the first time in the history of the human race a real man had lived, because for the first time a man had allowed the Creator God to live in him and control him utterly. And the strange thing is this, Jesus was so obviously not a prisoner, he was a truly free man. No one has ever been so liberated.

The 'freedom' Satan offered him would have left him chained as we are, a prisoner of his own ego, under the bondage of his own lusts. But Satan failed.

III THE NEW REALITY

The Death of Death

Three days after the crucifixion the disciples were seeing Jesus as even they had never seen him before. Always free in spirit and mind, he had in his lifetime inhabited a body subject to the same restrictions as any other human body in this falled world. Now that body raised from the dead was transformed. As solid as ever, it now passed from one scene to another at the will of Jesus without even the film-maker's favourite device of vague outline figure materialising and dematerialising. Here was total freedom and the disciples never forgot it or the promise that in the new heavenly kingdom they would have bodies like his.

The exuberant joy of his resurrection and the certainty of the coming kingdom could have sent them off round the world like rockets, and probably would have done if Jesus had not told them to wait. You see, he did not really want a repetition of that familiar human failing: a group of men discover a new spiritual truth, the excitement of it sends them into orbit, they turn it into good solid doctrine, reduce it to an intellectual system and return to earth with a bump. He knew it takes God to be a man. He had not come to earth, lived, died and risen just so that people could have a lot more things to talk about. He died and rose so that dying with him and rising with him by faith we could at last have the life of God in us, a permanent source of life and power.

Power from Above

That is why in the white-hot excitement of the days after the resurrection Jesus kept the disciples quiet. Just before he ascended he repeated that he wanted them to wait. 'For what?' we might ask. 'What more do they need?' And his reply would be, 'I came to bring them into the same relationship with my Father as I have always enjoyed.'

As they waited on the Father to keep his promise the plan of Jesus was working. Slowly they came to the point of rest, an attitude of quiet confidence in God. As the feast day of Pentecost dawned the floodgates of heaven were released and the Holy Spirit, the torrent of life that is the third person of the Trinity, poured into them. At last God had what he had been looking for – ordinary men who had received the life of God himself. The second Adam had left behind him a new kind of human being – not merely the product of human reproduction, whether conceived deliberately as a commitment to the future or in the heat of temporary passion. These were now children of God, born of his seed. For Jesus was placed by the Father in the womb of the earth to bring forth many sons of God whom he would be delighted to call 'my brothers'.

How did it happen to that rather dozy, quarrelsome bunch of misfits we now call 'the Apostles'? They received him and believed in his name. It was not that they committed themselves to an intellectual position, but they trusted everything they were and all they possessed on this:

Lord – he is God, his authority is absolute, we walk in obedience to him;

Jesus – he is God in sacrifice for our sins, winning forgiveness and freedom for us;

Christ – he is the promised King, the Man for whom all have waited, the one anointed with power from on high; living in us he gives us power to be different, the Holy Spirit who anointed him now comes to fill us.

Viewed in the person of Jesus Christ, Christianity

25

clearly works – beautifully. There is no fraud as long
as he remains, but if we dispense with him, then
Christianity becomes an empty container and the la-
bels on the outside promising peace, joy, fulfilment
and forgiveness become fraudulent claims, generating
deep bitterness in those who have been taken in. It
takes Christ to be a Christian as it takes God to be a
man. If a man or a woman has become a Christian –
that is, believing that Jesus Christ died for their sins
and rose again, they have allowed him to take up
residence in the centre of their lives – then God himself has made his home in that man's or that woman's
heart. Truly anything is possible to them, if they
believe.

The Crunch

And that is the crunch point – *if they believe*. Somehow
we have to find the humility to bow to the God of
Heaven, and tell him there are many things in his
book which we do not understand, and many others
which confuse us, but we really do accept its objective
truth and its reliability by faith. Somehow we have to
find the grace (it will not be difficult to find for grace
is never far away) to tell him that we have seen his
goodness, love, justice and joy in his Son and that we
commit ourselves in faith to that God forever. More
than that, we must take courage to believe he has
heard us and is now at home in our hearts. At his
invitation we have offered ourselves to him. He has
promised that in response the Father and the Son will
take up residence in our hearts, erecting there their
mighty throne. From that throne the water of life
flows, the Holy Spirit like a bubbling mountain
stream or a deep, majestic river, as Jesus promised he
would. If we take these propositions seriously then
we shall cease from our desperate search for God in

every new doctrine and sensation. Though we meet him in all sorts of places and in many different experiences we shall know that he is already in residence within.

If he truly lives in the centre of my being, what should my attitude be? Simply this: at the heart of me, something should lay prostrate in worship before him day and night. That is why Peter says, 'In your hearts set apart Christ as Lord.' Christ lives in my heart. It is a glorious, miraculous truth and if, confronted with this reality, we occasionally shout 'Hallelujah' or even 'Whoopee for Jesus' then it is, in my opinion, understandable.

'But how do we go on from this point?' asks the energetic, active sticker-covered modern Christian. Well, it really is quite simple. You go on as you started; trusting and worshipping the great God of all things who now lives *in* you, and let the Holy Spirit flow from you. That is all he has ever required.

The Quest of God

The Old Testament speaks of God's great search through thousands of years of history for men who would trust him sincerely. He was not looking for enormous intellect, gigantic physique, powers of leadership, oratory, or manufacture. He was looking for weak men with the guts to admit to him their weakness and to cling to him in total dependence. And he was doing it for just one reason; he loves men and delights to show his great might on their behalf.

'For the eyes of the Lord range throughout the earth to strengthen those whose hearts are fully committed to him.' (2 Chron. 16:9 NIV.)

'This is the man to whom I will look, he that is humble and contrite in spirit, and trembles at my word.' (Isa. 66:2 RSV.)

'I live in a high and holy place, but also with him who is contrite and lowly in spirit.' (Isa. 57:15 NIV.) When Jesus said 'Blessed are the pure in heart' (he meant those whose trust is not mixed with doubt) 'for they shall see God', he was only repeating the message of the (Jewish) Bible he held in his hand.

Later the search became more and more specific as God searched among his people for one man whose trust in God enabled him to stand in God's presence for the people of God. He asked Jeremiah to seek for one man who was honest and who was looking for truth. Ezekiel was told, 'I looked for a man among them who would build up the wall and stand before me in the gap on behalf of the land so I would not have to destroy it, but I found none.' (Ezek. 22:30 NIV.)

When Jesus came he was God's commitment in flesh to that continuing search, which is why he said, 'The Son of Man came to seek and to save what was lost.' As the discussion with the woman at the well-side drew to its close Jesus looked into the desperate, lonely face of the woman, now half believing, and won her heart with these words: 'A time is coming and has now come when the true worshippers will worship the Father in spirit and truth, for they are the kind of worshippers the Father seeks, (John 4:23 NIV). In her heart she decoded the message and got the truth: 'Imperfect in understanding as I am in everything else, God will still receive me if I give myself to him.'

A Brief Summary of the History of the World!
To summarise: the message so far is this . . . God has two purposes in making humanity, firstly to reveal himself and secondly to make man his governor for the earth and in the creation. Because of the activity

of Satan man's principal job as the executive of God's government in the earth was to be a defence and bulwark against the enemy. But the enemy seduced humanity and so penetrated the defences of God's creation government – turning the human race in rebellion against its original commander. This change is so fundamental in man that his natural state is one of enmity against God. He now hates and fears him and retreats from him whenever he meets him. But God comes looking for men and women just as he first sought Adam with the haunting words, 'Where are you?' Still God searches among men and women for those who will exercise, by choice, their right to be his children and when he finds anyone like this he restores them to their original function.

So now in this scene where the enemy who was outside is now inside, the strategy remains the same. Man will become the revelation of God's nature and government within creation and will accomplish his first purpose – the destruction of the whole rotten edifice of the kingdom of darkness. God has remained committed to this plan for two reasons: firstly he loves human beings and is not prepared to abandon them to the Satanic misery of Hell; secondly he will not be provoked into destroying the rebels by the exercise of his limitless power, for that would violate his own position as creator and sustainer. He is Love and in love became man himself, suffered and died, the innocent for the guilty, so that we the guilty could be freed from the bondage of Satan to whom we belonged as helpless slaves because of our sin. So we have become free people, dead to our old identities and possessors of new life, the children of the living God.

Learn from the Past

'He who will not learn from the past is condemned to repeat it' (George Santayana). God had a people before – the children of Israel. And his purpose for them was that they should be a priestly people. No, not that they should all wear dog collars! His plan was that the whole nation should stand for him before the people of the world – business men, carpenters, miners, foundry men, musicians, poets, dustmen, builders, all of them a revelation of God to the other nations. And as they carried that testimony to the four corners of the earth they would also be able to bear up those nations to God in prayer.

This fantastic strategy of a missionary nation depended on just one thing, the willingness of the Israelis to hear God's voice for themselves. But in a moment which was to be typical of their long history, they stood at Mount Sinai as the Lord God Almighty descended in fire and the whole mountain shook, and fear overcame them. They said to Moses, 'Speak to us yourself and we will listen. But do not have God speak to us or we will die' (Exod. 20:19 NIV). Israel's rejection at this moment of history was tragically to form the basis of their missing his revelation purpose. Later, as the Levitical priesthood arose, the human tendency to place God in a box marked 'Religious part of life' overpowered even this remarkable people. The whole story of the Jewish people has lasted thousands of years and to this day they are a mirror of the whole human race. In their story, all human stories can be seen – only more so.

The Radical Voice

So God sent to Israel his revolutionaries – the prophets. Their burden was the living God. Time and again they told the Israelis that God cannot be kept in the religious mould into which men tried to push him. He cannot be limited like that for he is God of all things, creator of all life. Again and again they reminded the Jews that God had called them to be a blessing to all peoples, and they promised that one day it would happen.

Then through an unknown called Joel he gave the most electrifying prophecy of all: 'And afterwards, I will pour out my Spirit on *all people*. Your sons and daughters will prophesy, your old men will dream dreams, your young men will see visions. Even on my servants, both men and women, I will pour out my Spirit in those days,' (Joel 2:28–29 NIV).

IV TERRIBLE AS AN ARMY WITH BANNERS

The Romantic Vision

So the vision was still there. God's people – a nation of ordinary people gathered from every racial, national, social, educational, tribal, occupational, and language group under heaven – all of them united more fundamentally than in any other relationship. What a dream: a worldwide community of people joined at the deepest level of being by the Spirit of God, united forever as brothers and sisters in the body of Christ. And most of them were to be ordinary working people, which is fitting and right because their King was a working man – born into the working class of his day.

In fact, for most of his adult life he fulfilled the Father's ordained function as a carpenter and in that trade he lived out the ancient inscription, 'Holy to the Lord'. Only three out of about twenty-one adult years were spent in preaching and teaching. In the rest of that time he glorified God, pleased his Father, earning his living as a manual worker. That was for us, for the millions of ordinary people who would follow him, working as taxi-drivers, milkmen, machine turners, dockers, policemen, farmers, butchers, clerks, bankers, teachers, brokers and even carpenters. 'Holy to the Lord' was inscribed on a golden plate which Aaron wore as part of his costume. That was not just for him, but for the whole Israeli people. They were a special people, set apart by God for a precisely designed function. And that is the way it is with us who are in Christ.

All creation is holy to the Lord because every last molecule is designed to fulfil his purpose. Here in the earth, as we have seen, that creation has been defiled by Satanic domination. So when Jesus prays for his disciples, 'Sanctify them' – make them holy – he is saying, 'Restore them to their original function. Only you as designer/maker God know what that function is.' Now he is not asking that they be made into weirdos, religious fanatics – he is asking for them to be restored to normality. God's norm for each one of us may be very different from the way we see ourselves, but he is the designer and maker of men and the one whose design programme has included everything that goes to make up the unique character that is you.

The Disciples' Prayer

So, for the character of the Almighty and Eternal God to be revealed in our world all God needs is a man or a woman, *any* man or woman will do. It is strange that the prayer Jesus gave to his disciples, which ought therefore to be called 'the disciples' prayer' is known worldwide as 'the Lord's prayer'. In that prayer he gave to us, as he gave to them, a guide to the right attitude in prayer. It begins in the warmth of a family relationship and a brief reminder of the greatness of the Father. But the real action comes when we say, 'Your kingdom come, your will be done', because that, if we mean it, is giving God absolute right to do anything he likes with me, my possessions, my relationships, anything. At some point it will inevitably mean suffering. We ought to be aware that it is a dangerous thing to say – the problem with God is that he takes you at your word.

But then widen the circle from your own concerns and pray, 'Your will be done' over the local community and the world scene. It introduces into the rebel world a new factor: the purpose of its maker and the reality of his power. It calls down into the fallen earth the Kingdom of Heaven. Both the world and the Church urgently need men and women who perceive this reality and live by it, and it is for them that God is continually looking.

The Weak and the Strong
I want to emphasise again that God's search is not for the self-sufficient strong man who needs nobody's help. In reality, of course, no such person exists; but many wear the mask of independent strength, sometimes even fooling themselves as well as others. Even within the Church people can be found strutting to centre stage, posturing like petty dictators. The mask of fascist power is a hard one for God to penetrate. The priority that Jesus gave to the downtrodden, the dispossessed and the diseased was an outworking of eternal reality.

God's search is still for people with hearts sincerely committed to him so that he can show his mighty power on their behalf. He seeks weak men and since all men are weak he seeks all men and all women. Any one of them will do. Notice I did not say he is looking for weaklings; the man or woman who runs away from reality, afraid to face the weakness within, perhaps even striking poses of heroic strength, is actually running from God. Such self-deception is the hardest thing of all for God to penetrate. So the Creator is searching for human beings who have faced themselves, recognised their weakness and will commit it to him. Those are the people who will know the power of God in their moral decisions, spiritual and emotional commitments, social contracts and worship. They will find that the one who made them delights to give himself in power to them. When Paul said, 'When I am weak, then I am strong', he was pointing to the deepest, profoundest and hardest lesson he had ever learned.

It takes guts to be weak before God. But when God finds a man or woman small enough to bless, then he really works overtime on their behalf. Hudson Taylor founded the mighty China Inland Mission. His vision and courage inspired a whole generation of the Church. But he did not look like a hero! He was a skinny man, subject to long bouts of melancholy. Asked for his secret he said, 'I think God was just looking for a man small enough to use, and he found me.'

Supermen or Sons and Saints
So this business is not about Nietzche's vision of the 'emerging superman' or Lenin's equally unattractive 'revolutionary man'. It *is* about ordinary people who make mistakes, lose their tempers, shout at their wives or husbands, lose their jobs, crash their cars, are afraid of the dentist, muddle their accounts and forget to spend time with God. In other words, it is about you and me; we are the ones for whom God has been looking all these years.

Maybe we have heard Murray McCheyne's saying:

'A holy man is an awesome weapon in the hands of Almighty God' and sighed, knowing that 'awesome' is the last word we would apply to ourselves. But we forget, we are the ones who have been called to the highest destiny of all. From before the foundation of the globe we have been set apart in the plan of the Maker, 'Holy to the Lord', for a task and function within a specific role. The extent to which we miss that function is the extent of our failure – our sin. You may feel that you have had such a bad start that you will never get anywhere. We forget that God specialises in taking the useless and making them useful, the failures and making them succeed, the weak and making them strong.

The apostle Paul's declaration of himself that he was the 'worst of sinners' has not stopped earnest Christians from romanticising him and thinking of him as a special case. The point he was making was that, if he was a special case, he was *typical* of the fact that to the God who loves us we are all special cases. Paul was called from his mother's womb to preach the gospel because that is the way God deals with us. He loves us and has called us all to a before-ordained purpose. We are Sons of God and called by him 'saints'.

An Army of Ordinary People
In the time of Jesus, it simply was not possible to buy from the local grocer a packet of pure salt. The salt he used was prepared by allowing sea water (often, but not only, from the Dead Sea) to flood a flat, shallow area of desert called a 'salt pan'. As the water evaporated it would leave behind a mixture of chemical salts, only part of which would be sodium chloride (salt). Because of this method of manufacture it was not pure salt and therefore it could lose its flavour

and become useless. When Jesus tells us, 'You are the salt of the earth', he is saying two things. Firstly, if the people of God are to do their job properly they must be spread through the earth, mixed with its peoples so as to permeate every part of human society. Secondly, when they have penetrated every part of society they must still have about them the distinctive flavour of the living god so that through them he can permeate the world of men with his presence. Salt that has lost its saltiness is just a handful of rubbish – thrown into the pot it will simply take on the flavour of the stew. The Christian who has lost his essential 'Godliness' will not permeate the world with God but will himself be saturated by the world around.

Now it must be obvious that Jesus' promise, 'You are the salt of the earth' cannot be fulfilled by the leaders of the Church, especially by its full-time servants. The promise can only be fulfilled by 'the people' of God. The vision is an army of ordinary people who have made themselves available to the extraordinary God who made them, so that they no longer live by their own power. They know they are weak and have given it to him. So they live by his indwelling power and, by the quality of their human lives, they witness to his reality and undying love.

Total Frustration
It is as simple as that! And as difficult. It is a daily struggle to allow Jesus to live through us the unique expression of himself, which is why he made us. We all know the frustration of Paul: 'I do not understand what I do. For what I want to do I do not do, but what I hate I do, (Rom. 7:15. NIV). No wonder he says, 'What a wretched man I am! Who will rescue me from this body of death?' The answer to the question is not given. Paul simply gives thanks – the

moment of total frustration is the moment of God's opportunity – then he can give us himself as never before.

It is not a question of attempting self-improvement by applying religious rules and regulations. Such things appear to help, but are not truly any good at combating sin, raising the standard of righteousness or increasing the flow of holy life. The real power is in God himself and the miracle is that he has come to live in those who are committed to Jesus Christ. So the power we need is already within us. What must we do to draw on it? We must worship him in our hearts and abandon all pretence that we can manage without him. Then we must allow him to move out in his kingly power from the centre of our lives to the outer edges. This is the work of a moment. Learning it as a permanent attitude is the work of a lifetime.

I would like to summarise all I have said so far:

(i) Put yourself in God's hands without any reservation.

(ii) Follow obediently all his commands, relying on the fact that Jesus Christ lives in you.

(iii) Let the Holy Spirit fill you and give you power, and

(iv) You will find that *God can use you.*

The Impact

If our generation in the Church of the Western World were truly to commit itself to full surrender to Christ, total dependence on God, the truth of the Bible, honest prayer, and the power of the Holy Spirit, we would have the radiant beauty of God and, like Solomon's bride, be 'terrible as an army with banners' (S. of S. 6:10 RSV). There is no doubt that society would feel the impact, an impact that would come through millions of day-to-day contacts with people at work, in the markets and shops, and in family homes. However, this almost totally private impact is not all we should be aiming at.

V A HIGHWAY FOR OUR GOD

The Rich and Greedy

God is looking for people who will challenge the values of the world around. From us he wants a voice that will remind people in our frantic money-mad western society that the world is not theirs but his, and since they are living handsomely off his riches he requires them to rightly distribute his resources. If we are to do that we will need to be absolutely sure that we have faced the implication of our message. We must ourselves be people who are not dominated by money and who sit very lightly to our possessions.

For we must be unafraid to challenge the status quo, unafraid to go to government and power structures, large corporations and say, 'People matter more than things.' It is time we proclaimed loud and clear that our governmental obsession with the Gross National Product and the value of our currency, is idolatry. It is time we brought to the attention of society that higher productivity may actually be counter-productive, if it means that limited material resources are being used up faster than possible alternatives can be developed. And if it means that, the whole social fabric of society begins to collapse, because higher productivity actually means fewer participating members with the rest on an increasingly huge scrap-heap; then the state itself can collapse.

To use natural resources as we are doing wantonly and frivolously is irresponsible stewardship. And when it comes to alternatives we are just as irresponsible. For instance, nuclear power has a tremendous God-given potential for the energy hungry world. But it also has a ghastly potential for unimaginable harm if we do not find a method of dealing with the waste so as to render it harmless. To proliferate piles of waste that may be lethal for thousands of years is madness.

We *are* stewards, and one day THE OWNER is coming back to judge our stewardship. To squander human beings as we are doing for financial gain is blasphemy and the MAKER will judge us for it.

The world must hear the warning voice that cries out of judgement to come. We must learn to see people and to judge events from the perspective of eternity. The world needs people who are able to make decisions not based on terrible fear and panic but on confidence in God. All over the western world the level of confidence felt in our institutions is falling. Extremists of left and right battle for control, proclaiming their infallible answers. Fear rises and factions increase in number as people refuse to trust anyone but their own man. The rise of protectionism born of fear will inexorably produce what it most fears. The fear of economic slump will produce it.

The Poor and Needy

Our western civilization is under judgement because like the civilizations of the past, it rides on the backs of the slave population of the world. God cares about the people of the so-called Third World.

The world need is for clear-eyed messengers who will say, 'The economy of the world cannot always expand. The mad consumerism of the past half-century is a historical quirk. Indeed the economy *should not* expand as it has. What has happened is that the rich have got richer and so have the poor, but not as quickly as the rich. So the poor are now even poorer. There are great pockets of dire poverty and extreme scarcity of food, while here in the West we throw away more food than we consume. This is not acceptable to the God who made all the earth.' Not that we doubt the saying of Jesus, 'The poor you always have with you', but there is no evidence that he said it with calm or placid acceptance. We who know him have no doubt he said it with grief and pain in his heart. So we must be a priestly people standing between an angry God and a feckless people, pleading with him *for* them and proclaiming him *to* them.

The Place to Stand
The eyes of the Lord still range across the earth, seeking for men and women who will stand with him and for him. If we are to speak in power to our society, we need a revived people in the Church who stand in a right position with God because they have forgotten smaller ambitions in the burning desire to *know* God and make him known. Instead of agreement on the lowest level, we need to be committed to the highest in ourselves and with each other.

The Last Enemy
People who give themselves to the will of God have become part of his alternative society, his Church, and the Church is the earthly arm of the Kingdom of Heaven. It has its own values and principles and above all it has the total confidence that one day that kingdom will reign over all things. So death itself is only the door to the Kingdom of God. In a world more and more obsessed with avoiding death, we who know the one who once was dead and is now alive forever have a message to proclaim by the way we die. We have no fear of death. We die triumphantly – it is our greatest testimony.

Listen to people talk as they grow old. Weary, dragging feet belong to those who look back to the good old days, but eager feet press forward knowing that through death is the best – Jesus himself. Our world needs that message. If we are to convince them, then we ourselves must be sure that we are definitely going somewhere. As a pilgrim people we demonstrate to an aimlessly wandering world that there is a destination; we march purposefully to the Beautiful City. The great Kingdom of Heaven lies before us. In that kingdom the whole romance of history and creation will be consummated, as we all who belong to Christ, made one at last in the great body of the Church, will as the Bride be joined to Christ for ever. Then we start the real story – an eternal love story.

Now this may seem the classic 'pie in the sky when you die' line but it is the most practical doctrine in the Christian faith. It sets God's people free to live without fear and thus to confront evil with a confidence no other people can match.

The Bomb

So when we say that the nuclear arms race is evil, wicked and diabolical we are speaking literally, not from fear. The modern peace movement is basically a fear movement and Christians cannot identify themselves with institutional fear, because their basis is confidence in God. So we can face the issues clearly. We must say that, ultimately, God is our defence. Now there are debates within the Church on the whole issue of war and peace and there are great disagreements, but on this issue there is a large measure of agreement. To say that my freedom to live in a certain way should be defended by the deaths of countless millions of non-combatants in another country is totally unacceptable. Any person who believes that Jesus was raised from the dead as a fore-runner for all

41

who trust in him would rather die than have such a burden on his conscience.

Of course it is possible that a decision not to use nuclear arms would mean our society being overrun by an enemy. For the Church of Jesus Christ this would only mean a return to normality. The vast majority of the Church has always had to live and witness under pressure, sometimes active persecution.

Now I am aware that this is only a sketchy coverage of the peace debate. What I want to emphasise is that confidence in God enables us to face such issues clearly. Our assurance of the total reality of heaven and its ultimate triumph gives us a uniquely objective view-point.

Set Yourself Apart

When the voice of God says to us 'Sanctify yourself' he is saying 'Set yourself apart to fulfil the function for which I, your designer, intended you.' The whole creation is his and all that is in it. It all belongs to him. Its politics, its money, its business and social structures, governments and huge international con-glomerates – all are his! All of them are also in rebellion against him. Our task therefore is to move out in the power of the Holy Spirit to bring all of life under the authority of Jesus Christ. Whatever we do, whether emptying dustbins or operating on brains, we work for him and as we give him all we do we sanctify it. We are agents of another king and another kingdom, and we cannot be beaten because we know that one day the kingdom of the world will become the kingdom of our God and of his Christ. Few un-derstand that we are the most dangerous people on earth! The living God will one day sit on the throne of every kingdom and government in the world and the programme to bring that about has been placed in the hands of the Church. But for that to happen, God needs *you*.

A man called D. L. Moody once heard someone say, 'The world has yet to see what God can do with one man who is completely yielded to him.' The words went deep into his heart and the response came, 'By God's grace I will be that man.' His voice had a high nasal twang. He could not spell and knew hardly any grammar. In the last letter he ever wrote there were thirty-eight spelling mistakes and grammatical errors. He became the greatest evangelist the world had ever seen. Some even said he was the greatest man of the nineteenth century.

God offers you a chance to be a hero. Why would you settle for anything less? You may not necessarily be famous, but earthly fame is a shadow, an illusion. The real fame is heavenly and eternal. 'Blessed are the dead who die in the Lord from now on . . . for their deeds will follow them' (Rev. 14:13 NIV).

If you are willing to offer yourself in service to the King – he will accept you. If you are willing to surrender all earthly dreams and live for the Heavenly Kingdom *God can use you.*

PART TWO
THE ANSWER

1: Personal Surrender

Dressed in sweater and jeans, she calmly sauntered down the High Street, early twenties, blonde, and attractive enough to turn a few heads. She seemed an ordinary enough girl with all the sophistication expected by the 1980s. One thing stood out – the badge on her sweater which proudly announced:

'Look after yourself.'

This sounds ordinary enough. But that's just the problem. It is the view-point of most people. 'Look after yourself; after all, if you don't, no one else will!'

One of the reasons why Jesus always caused so many problems for ordinary people who examined his life, is that he demonstrated a perfect alternative to their way of living. Instead of trying to get his own way, Jesus found his greatest satisfaction in doing his Father's will. Rather than live for himself, Jesus devoted his life to helping others. For the first time since the Garden of Eden the life-style of the Kingdom of God, that had once been lived by Adam, was re-introduced among ordinary men and women. 'The Word became flesh and lived for a while among us . . . the one and only [Son]' (John 1:14 NIV).

Jesus' words were backed up by his life. He came announcing 'the good news of the kingdom' (Luke 4:43), re-introducing the concept which governed the whole of the Old Testament from the Garden of Eden to the Roman invasion of Palestine. In Genesis we see that God created man and woman with a unique dimension which set them apart from the whole of the rest of creation. 'So God created man in his own image' (Gen. 1:27). Adam and Eve were designed to live in harmony with God, with each other, and with the rest of the created world. They were to look after the whole of creation with love and respect, and could walk and talk with God himself.

The whole of creation is included in God's Kingdom. After all, it owed its genesis to his creative energy. All lived and related together in perfect accord with the will of God. Then an unwise angel named Satan grew proud of his own power and tried to challenge the authority of the will of God. He claimed the right for angels and men alike to live their own way independent of the will of God.

Disaster followed . . . This picture of peace was smashed by war in heaven which soon spread down to earth. When man followed Satan's disobedience he broke away from the will of God. Chaos and broken relationships have existed on earth ever since that moment when men and women chose the kingdom of Satan rather than the Kingdom of God.

This choice came from the simple suggestion that men and women are independent beings with the authority to direct and determine their own destiny. Instead, the Bible suggests that mankind has a unique potential and destiny. In other words, we are uniquely designed to live as children of the living God, knowing, loving and obeying him.

Britain in the mid-1980s lies in the grip of spiritual warfare, each of us belonging either in the Kingdom of God or the kingdom of Satan. There is no middle ground: despite the ideas that many of us have, we cannot be spiritually neutral. Many would be horrified to realise that if you are wandering undirected, following your pleasures, career, money, or doing anything for your own sake, you are in fact siding with Satan and struggling against God and against his people.

God teaches us what it means to be surrendered to his Kingdom through the history of Israel. The Bible vividly describes people in unique relationship with God for as long as they trusted and obeyed him. Time and again Satan encouraged their rebellion and disobedience, and tried to overthrow the demonstration of the Kingdom, until a battered and bruised nation limped into three captivities, Assyria, Babylon, and finally a Roman-dominated Palestine. Instead of being known as the nation of God, loved and cared for by him, her continual rebellion made Israel a laughing stock, so that Joel cried, 'Why should they say among the peoples, "Where is their God?" ' (Joel 2:17 NIV). To cover their shame, national and religious leaders developed the hope of a coming day of the Lord, when the Kingdom would be introduced as a political reality and the Romans overthrown. In the spiritual poverty of our nation many similarly pin their hopes on a future Kingdom when Jesus returns, as of course he certainly will!

We, like Israel, are in danger of missing the point. Of course the final completion of the Kingdom lies in the future, but with the birth of a baby in a Bethlehem cowshed the new age of the Kingdom was inaugurated.

And so came Jesus, God's very own Son, as someone to demonstrate his Kingdom. He fulfilled all considerations, political, social, economic, and spiritual. He lived for others as he proclaimed the needs for social justice, in a life of love where he healed the sick, fed the hungry and brought the life of God to ordinary men and women. In his life he showed the Kingdom; in his death he opened the possibility of living in that Kingdom, and when he returns he will complete that Kingdom.

On the cross Jesus showed the most perfect example of obedience in his perfect surrender to the will of God; an obedience which contrasts so vividly with our own reluctance to follow any direction other than our own.

As if his own example was not enough, Jesus also left us his own statement of the Kingdom, as it relates to us as individuals, in his prayer for disciples. In a style typical of his times, Jesus repeats himself. 'Thy Kingdom come' is clarified by, 'Thy will be done on earth as it is in heaven.' The Kingdom is no longer expressed by a nation; now it consists of individuals, but individuals who have committed their lives and life-styles to a king other than themselves.

Jesus said, 'No one can be a slave of two masters; he will hate one and love the other; he will be loyal to one and despise the other. You cannot serve both God and money' (Matt. 6:24 GNB). There is only ever room for one king in a kingdom. The tragedy of many Christian lives is that we try to have two! The central point of the Christian message is that Jesus came to liberate us from having to live for ourselves. Instead of trying to do good in our own strength, we can be released to live in the power and authority of the Christ who comes to live within us by his indwelling Holy Spirit.

Man's kingdom says, 'You rule your life – do your own thing.' God wants individuals living in his Kingdom who will allow him to dictate their habits and life-styles. He searches for those who will abdicate the thrones of their own lives and step down so that he may come and reign as Lord and King.

The non-Christian is at least honest; he lives for himself and knows it. Many of us who claim to know and love Jesus seem to believe that we are permitted to live our own lives providing we add on Bible-reading, praying and church-going for God's benefit. We try to confine God's activity within us to very few areas of our lives, so that often he is left with our 'Sundays and the dog-ends of our time.' We have our own ideas and ambitions, our own money and possessions, our own time-table and commitments. But Jesus wants far more from us than partnership – he desires total ownership. Not because he takes delight in depriving us of personality or initiative. Far from it; he longs to make us into all that we can be when reunited with God himself. The appalling defects introduced by Satanic rule can disappear in the redeeming life and love which Jesus brings.

Why then has Christianity become a happy hobby? A nice extra to know that Jesus has forgiven you? We certainly dress for him, and go to meetings but little else seems to result from our faith. We play the Christian game with our pattern of activities, magazines, records, etc., but we carefully avoid the world which Jesus died for, just in case we might be polluted and frightened by it. We wear his name but know in our hearts that we are unprepared to give all our lives to the one who gave all his life for us.

Often our spiritual poverty is illuminated when we contrast the depth of our commitment to Jesus with that of the adherents of a political creed or ideal:

'In 1954 a missionary in Vietnam was told by a Viet Cong guerilla officer, "I would gladly die if I could advance the cause of Communism one more mile . . . You know, as you have read to me from the Bible I have come to believe that you Christians have a greater message than that of Communism.

But I believe that we are going to win the world, for Christianity means something to you, but Communism means everything to us." It is just that kind of passionate, disciplined, sacrificial commitment which Jesus preached we should have, but many are aware that it is just this which we have lost.'[1]

The root of the problem lies in our will, or lack of it!

For many of us our wills act as useful valves to control the amount of commitment we are really prepared to offer to Jesus. Time and again our will comes up against the desires of God for our lives. When our will crosses his revealed will and we surrender, then we are truly experiencing Kingdom lives. Just as Jesus surrendered to the will of his Father in the Garden of Gethsemane, so he wants our surrender to him. This is not just a once and for all thing but an ongoing process. Time and again we will discover a part of our lives in which the will of God crosses our desires. It is at this point that our will must turn round to conform to that of our Lord!

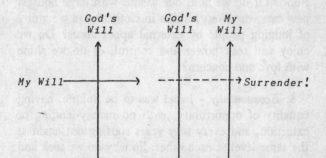

For Israel, four thousand years ago, the dilemma was exactly the same as it is for us as individuals today. Do we live by our own standards or by the revealed will of God? Israel's choice was the same and in her case God's demands were overlooked or ignored so often that recurring judgment was inevitable. His requirement that Israel should be different to the other nations, a true alternative society, was simple and just, and his claims on the Church are exactly the same.

1. *Politically* – Israel was to be unique, with no ultimate king or ruler but God himself. For ourselves, who do we look to? Who are we influenced by? Do we believe that the GLC, the Prime Minister, the USA controls events – or God himself?

2. *Socially* – Israel was to be unique, an example of social concern, committed to the poor, needy, widowed and orphaned; ruled by justice, peace and love, with no slaves or elaborate social heirachy. For our part, do we give to the poor, Help the Aged, Tear Fund? Or do we flout our wealth with large houses, new cars, the latest fashion in clothes? Are we guilty of judging people by external appearances? Do we enjoy and seek power and control, or do we shine with love and concern?

3. *Economically* – Israel was to be unique, having equality of opportunity, with no money-lending or extortion, and every fifty years starting out again at the same level as each other. So why do we seek and plan for continued success in our careers? In our own lives would we be prepared to be reduced to the same level as others and to start out from scratch? Are we prepared to suffer in order that others may be helped?

4. *Spiritually* – they were to be unique, serving and worshipping the living God as his own people, and in right relationships with each other. Personally we must ask if God is our first and overwhelming priority. Do we discipline our lives to give time to God? Do we worship him, or ourselves?

In these, as in so many other areas, it is the will which is the crucial factor. Some of us make deliberate decisions against the will of God by choice. Far more often the Christian is not actively driving off in the wrong direction. Instead we lack a motor, or wheels, in the first place. Apathy, fantasy, a preparedness to settle for second-best. These are all sins which we need to surrender to the Lord.

How impatient we become that there is no quick, easy experience of conforming to the will of God! But we must surrender day by day. As A. W. Tozer has pointed out:

> 'The most advanced soul may be shocked and chagrined to discover some private area in his life where he had been, unknown to himself, acting as Lord and proprietor of that which he thought he had given to God. It is the work of the in-living Spirit to point out these moral discrepancies and correct them. He does not, as it is sometimes said, "break" the human will, but he does invade it and bring it gently to a joyous union with the will of God.'[2]

Why are God's demands so absolute? Surely he is no arbitrary demagogue demanding our subservience? What can we add to God himself? The answer is that we can add nothing to God; he desires our commitment for what he can add to us, not the other way round.

The Steps to Personal Surrender

a) *Recognise our own weaknesses* – lack of words, actions, love, godly living. God does not just sit back and make demands of us. He wants our wills surrendered to him in order that he might bring his words, actions, love, life-style to us. The last thing God wants is for us to try to be better in ourselves. Rather, he wants our surrender in order that he might come to us to provide all that we need.

b) *Recognise our sin-sick society and our own personal need*, our disregard of God, his Kingdom and the good news. We are the hands and feet of Jesus, the means to fulfil his life on earth, to do his work. But the individual parts of the body need direction from the brain. In the same way, unless our lives are under the direction of Jesus, we will be as unco-ordinated and disjointed as our arm 'doing its own thing'. If God is to reach our nation, we must live under his directive will alone!

c) *Recognise our own need to be loved and accepted.* The Father wants us as his children, sons of God and joint-heirs with Jesus. True sonship only exists in direct obedience to a divine Fatherhood. Jesus said 'I can do nothing on my own authority; I judge only as God tells me, so my judgment is right, because I am not trying to do what I want, but only what he who sent me wants' (John 5:30 GNB). As we do the will of God we really live as his sons, relaxing into his love and purposes.

d) *Recognise our need to commit ourselves to following Jesus*, and receiving his life and power to do so. From that moment on we need to discover in the Bible and prayer our ongoing communication with God himself.

e) *Recognise that God knows us better than we know ourselves*, because he is the creator. He has a way for our lives which is different to any which we can imagine. Many of us live with the misconception that God wants from us all that we don't want to give, and that his way is always painfully unpleasant! Now Jesus never promised us an easy ride, but in doing his will we so often find that his way for our lives is ten times better than our wildest dreams!

As Michaelangelo once patiently chipped away at a fat, ugly block of marble onlookers found it difficult to believe his claim that locked inside was a beautiful angel. Months later his patience was rewarded. In the same way God is patiently dealing with us, chipping away until our wills bend to his. We also require patience; the Christian life isn't achieved in a moment. As I once read on the jeans' patch of a young Christian, 'Please have patience, God hasn't finished dealing with me yet!'

So much of the reality of our surrender depends on the depth of our relationship with God. For it is only as we spend time with God, learning to know him and discern his desires for our lives, that we discover all that the Lord wants our surrender to mean.

It is easy to give up; to believe Satan's lie that our stubborn will can never conform to that of the Lord. We look at spiritual superstars and fail to see their feet of clay. We wonder how we can ever achieve their spiritual stature, without realising that they too are still growing and developing with God, just as we are. We remember our failings and failures without realising that God has always taken on those who have failed, because to them he can demonstrate his love and forgiveness. Peter denied Jesus. He must have found it difficult to live with the shame, but he became a man after God's heart who pioneered the good news to the Jews scattered worldwide.

Elijah, Moses, the list goes on and on of those who

knew the bitterness of failure. Yet God went on to forgive and love and use them. That did not mean that he condoned their actions but rather that he met them in their failure. Mark carefully noted that Jesus loved the rich young ruler, and for this reason he challenged the young man to surrender at the very place where it would hurt him most – his wealth. His defiance of the will of God meant that he went away from Jesus a desperately unhappy man.

In Genesis chapter 32 verses 22 to 32, we read an important story. Jacob, a cheat and a failure, arrived at the ford of the Jabbok river. For two-thirds of his life he had trusted in his own strength to determine his destiny. That night he was alone. In God's time-table there will always come a time when we are left alone, and that will often be the moment for meeting with God. The Lord came as a man to wrestle with Jacob. To convince him that his natural strength was not enough. Time and again Jacob tried to assert himself just as he had in his life. He survived the night but at dawn God put his thigh out of joint. In Hosea chapter 12 verse 4 we read that Jacob 'fought against an angel and won. He wept and asked for a blessing.' Jacob won! He won by being beaten by God and so will we. We win in life by yielding to God and his direction. Jacob left that place limping, and all his life he bore that mark of his battle with God. It's better to give in while we're in one piece, but even so there will be unmistakable evidences in our daily lives that we have encountered the living God and are being daily mastered by him.

Jacob gained his victory when he pleaded for bless-ing in his life with the God who had defeated him. God gave blessing, as he always does. He turned Ja-cob's life around, taking the stubborn and self-willed rebel and making him into a meek and dignified friend of God.

When we come in weakness day by day to God, confessing that we can never change ourselves and pleading for his hand on our lives, then we will never be turned down. It is only into our self-acknowledged weakness that God can pour his strength. He loves the cry of conquered men and women whose wills he can mould and whose lives he can fill! We may never arrive at a Jabbok but we can meet God where we are if we come in weakness pleading for him and discovering that the life-transforming power which Jacob encountered is still the same today.

Coming to God in weakness and surrender is itself an act of the will. Many of us need to plead with the Lord to hold up a divine mirror in front of us, that we may see our desperate need and turn to him. We long to get to God by our own efforts instead of by the only way of simple surrender to his love.

When we rest in the arms of God, as a child in the arms of his father, then we begin to understand the direction, purpose and power of the Christian life.

Watchman Nee tells the story of how he and a friend were walking by a lake when they heard the screams of someone drowning. Because his friend was a far superior swimmer, Nee waited for him to dive in. Meanwhile the drowning man went under for the second time! Only when he submerged the third time did Nee's friend swim over and complete the rescue. When asked why he took so long about it, he coolly replied, 'I had to wait until he'd gone under three times; only then would he stop struggling.'

Only when we have given up hope of achieving the will of God through our own efforts will we surrender into his arms instead.

Many of us choose to opt out of the struggle altogether. We conform to the norms and values of the world around us and try to be the same as everybody else. Bright has aptly commented:

'The carnal Christian . . . tries to live the Christian life in his own effort, rather than trusting in the indwelling Christ, for he does not know how to stop being carnal and to again become spiritual . . . From thousands of surveys taken all over the world approximately 95% of all professing Christians identify themselves as carnal, not because they want to be carnal but because they do not know how to be spiritual.'

Compromise is everywhere, but we rarely recognise it. We endeavour to make everyone feel happy and at ease without realising that some things are just not negotiable. Jesus called us to live under his will and authority rather than our own. Such is the essence of the Kingdom.

In Korea the story is often told of those who stood in positions of leadership, but failed to avoid compromise when the communists arrived with their demands of compulsory atheism. One of dozens of illustrations of how ordinary Christians put their leaders to shame is this one:

When the communists arrived in the north they tried to destroy Christianity in the village areas. Soldiers would gather the population into the church building, tear down a picture of Jesus, place it at the front of the church and demand that the people spit on the picture of jesus Christ. Then they would be free.

In one small church the senior clergyman thought of his parishioners and the need to go on preaching to them and spat on the picture. After all he needed to be free, and it was only a picture! Then his colleague followed suit. A young Christian girl went forward, took the picture and gently wiped the spittle away with the hem of her skirt while she spoke of her love for Jesus and all he had done for her. The soldiers were so moved by her devotion to Jesus that they shot the clergy who so easily denied their Lord and spared the people!

It is so difficult to know what we would do in a crisis. Two things are certain. The world is not impressed by an easy-going, compromising faith. If we want to make it with the Lord through the big things, we have to practise setting our will to agree with his in the small things! The more used we become to doing the will of God in small matters, the stronger we can be in the crises.

'The will, not the feelings, determines moral direction. The root of all evil in human nature is the corruption of the will. The prodigal son took his first step upward from the pig-sty when he said, "I will arise and go to my father." As he had once willed to leave his father's home now he willed to return.'

It is as we turn to Jesus in surrender that he draws us lovingly to himself and begins that gentle taming of our will which alone can transform our lives. It is only then that Jesus can achieve that total invasion where he can bring to us all that we need to live his life and be his people. The Christian life is never one of trying to do the will of God, but always of simple surrender so that he can come to do his will in us! As we read in Amos chapter 3 verse 3 (AV), 'Can two walk together, except they be agreed.' How can we walk with Jesus unless our wills are in harmony with his?

The old story is told of a French admiral, defeated by Lord Nelson in naval combat, meeting Nelson and offering a respectful handshake. He was told, 'Your sword first, sir, then your hand.' We cannot meet the King of Kings as an equal; if we want to know God we must first surrender our wills to him so that he can make real that deep relationship within our lives which we long for. Such a life begins by conquest, the King of Kings restoring us to the life of the Garden, of the Kingdom, where he reigns over us and we walk with him.

Malcolm Muggeridge recognised the need for radical reorientation of our lives, from self-existence to the life-style of Kingdom, when he wrote these words:

'So I come back to where I began, to that other King, one Jesus; to the Christian notion that man's efforts to make himself personally and collectively happy in earthly terms are doomed to failure. He must indeed, as Christ said, be born again, be as a new man or he's nothing. So at least I have concluded, having failed to find in the past experience, present dilemmas and future expectations, any alternative proposition. As far as I am concerned, "it is Christ or nothing".'[3]

2: Prayer

Prayer is the most intimate thing we do. It is the pursuit of a relationship before it is anything else. That is its purpose.

I PRIVATE PRAYER – CONSTANT SHARING

It is Natural
Prayer is the personal intercourse of two friends – God and man walking together. It is the sharing of life and self between lovers. Just as the Bible says of Adam that 'he knew Eve his wife' in sexual intercourse, so in prayer man and God came to know each other in the most intimate and personal way. Thus prayer is the most natural activity for the Christian – as natural as breathing, and like breathing it still works!

Then why do so many people find it a problem – why for instance did one new Christian say to me 'Prayer is hard, isn't it?' In the end, the reason is that our enemy, Satan, fears prayer more than anything else we ever do, so he works to surround it with difficulties of every kind.

This above all – Be True
The most common difficulty is the feeling that somehow I must get myself ready to pray: the spiritual

equivalent of putting on my best clothes, polishing my shoes, combing my hair for a particularly demanding interview. But God is not a prospective employer or Great-aunt Matilda. He made us to be perfect and knows all our faults better than we do. Trying to clean up in order to face him is not only a waste of time, it is plain silly. Like a small boy who has been playing in a ditch all morning and then vainly tries to clean off the mud with his handkerchief, we fool nobody. Only one thing makes us ready for prayer: praying. Simply come as you are. That is the meaning of the grace of God; he accepts you as you are and only asks that you do the same – admit to yourself and him what you are. Honesty is what he asks for. Be ruthless with yourself, always be absolutely honest with him. God can do nothing with your lies but he will use the truth no matter how bad it may be.

Be Natural

Another difficulty is the feeling that since God is so much higher and holier than we are we should take a special posture and use special language to speak to him. But a moment's thought will show that this is foolish. We are talking about the most natural and delightful activity in the world – two lovers sharing their lives together. Using a special formal language, particularly an ancient pattern like sixteenth century English, would make the relationship strained and unnatural. And prayer is the most natural activity for a Christian – so do it naturally. Use your own language and pray at all times. Share your life with your heavenly lover: after all, he died a terrible death to win you so that he could be joined in love to you forever. Whatever you are doing and all you feel, is interesting to him. Always and everywhere talk to him: at work, in the car, train or plane, in the bathroom, kitchen or chapel, country lane or intercity highway. Share your reactions with him *first*. 'He died for us so that whether we are awake or asleep we may live together with him' (I Thessalonians 5 v. 10)

Let Him Share With You
But remember that living together with him means you not only talk to him, you listen to him. And as you share with him your view of the world he will show you the way he sees it. Often that will bring you great pain; there is no suffering anywhere in the world that God does not feel most of all. Jesus knows it because he carried it all at Calvary. So he will share it with you, to drive you to prayer. As you speak to him, he will lead you to the heavenly Father to ask *him* to act. For God has given the world to man, placing it under his authority. And this means he requires our prayers to change things. John Wesley said 'God does nothing in this world except by prayer.' So as you see things in the world around that need changing, don't just groan and grumble or turn away, trying to forget – pray, pray and pray again that our Almighty Father will release his power and change those things as he wants to. So sharing life with Jesus is only one aspect of prayer. The Bible describes him as our elder brother and his purpose is to lead us to his Father so that we know and enjoy the Heavenly Father as he does, joining our wills to his in determination that his kingdom will come to our world.

Know Who You Pray To
The three-in-one nature of God can be another diffi-culty in prayer, because some Christians are confused about which member of the trinity they should pray to. Put most simply we pray to the Father through

the Son by the power and guidance of the Holy Spirit. Yet many Christians find it hard to pray to the Father, for them it is easier to identify with Jesus, so they pray to Jesus all the time, even when asking for the kind of action that is the work of the Father-Creator. Usually this is because they have had little or no relationship with their earthly father. If this is a problem for you, remember: firstly, Jesus is our great go-between, any prayer you direct to him that asks for the action of the Father is sent on by him to the Father. Secondly, the Father is Jesus' own Father and he called him "Abba" – "Dad". Since the great heavenly Father is your best friend's Dad, you have no reason to be afraid. Thirdly, because of Jesus the Heavenly Father has become your "Dad" too. If you have never really grasped this, then start to do it now by faith; just as you received Jesus as your Saviour by faith, reach out and receive the heavenly Father as your own father. As you do this you will find it more and more natural to pray to him about everything that concerns you.

Having said this, the New Testament makes it clear that prayer can be addressed to the Father, Son, or Holy Spirit, though prayer to the Holy Spirit is fairly unusual. The reason for this is that he is the one who actually inspires and empowers our prayers.

Where Is He?

My three year old daughter asked the question 'Is Jesus in this room, Daddy?'. 'Yes, he certainly is.' 'Well, I looked everywhere for him and didn't see him. Is he under the bed or in the cupboard? Where is he?' I searched for the right words as parents have always done. How do you explain the immanence, the 'everywhereness' of the invisible God to a three year old . . . or to a thirty-three year old? All we can ever do is affirm that it is so – wherever we go, he is there, whether we search the depths of the sea or out into the galaxies, he is there, Love himself awaits us everywhere. So there are no restrictions on where we pray. God hears it all whether it comes from prison cell, palace throne room, living room, company board room or church. However, many of us make a great mistake when we forget that of all places, God is most at home in *us*. The fact is that when we turn in faith to the son of God, committing ourselves totally to his will, the new birth he works in us restores us to our original purpose. We were made for God himself to live in us and when we give ourselves to him he gladly comes to take up residence in us. What a privilege – we are the temple of the living God. He dwells in us.

So the first place we should seek him is in our hearts. It is our blood-bought privilege, the inheritance of every ordinary member of the Body of Christ. If you are in Christ, God lives in you so that you can know him and share quiet intimacy with him. So turn confidently within in prayer, your God *will* meet you there in your spirit, at your centre. For he has become your centre; Festo Kivengere rightly says 'The man without Christ is a man without a centre.' So in our hearts, at the centre where he dwells should always be a place of awe where a part of us is bowed in worship. Into our failing, faltering humanity, God has come. Seek him in his temple: 'that temple you are.' He will meet you there. If you are truly a Christian, Christ dwells in your heart by faith; he waits for you there. Go in to meet him.

II PRIVATE PRAYER – DELIBERATE CARING

We began by considering prayer as the instant and spontaneous sharing of life with the Lord Jesus and the Father. We now turn to think about prayer as a deliberate act. We all need to spend time in the presence of God, time when he is the whole focus of our attention. The most helpful way to arrange this is to pick a time when we will be undisturbed (if necessary we must make sure that we will not be disturbed). Watching Jesus, as he frequently took periods out of his busy schedule to spend time with his Father in prayer, the disciples felt as we do, 'I wish I could do that'. Looking at him as he emerged, refreshed, from these times, they envied him and asked, 'Lord, teach us to pray.'

The words he spoke in answer are recorded in Matthew 6 v.5–15. (NIV). They form the most valuable and concise teaching on prayer ever given.

V.5 **'But when you pray, do not be like the hypocrites for they love to pray, standing in the synagogues and on the street corners to be seen by men. I tell you the truth, they have received their reward in full.'** In Jesus' day, many Pharisees practised 'private' prayer on the street for effect. Jesus said, 'don't make a display of your private prayer or you will get no answer from God – the only answer you will get is from the crowd around, not much use.'

V.6 **'When you pray, go into your room, close the door and pray to your Father who is unseen. Then your Father who sees what is done in secret will reward you.'** Here he says, 'Take seriously the relationship you have with your Father. His love for you is exclusive; there are times when he wants you all to himself, so give yourself the right circumstances. Be alone with him, be private and keep what you share with him to yourself. This is the power of effective prayer.' Keep it secret till he answers. By the way, Jesus himself sometimes found privacy for prayer by walking alone in the hills – many of us still find this a valuable alternative to the private room.

V.7–8 'And when you pray, do not keep on babbling like pagans, for they think they will be heard because of their many words. Do not be like them for your Father knows what you need before you ask him.' Notice the very strong repetitions of the phrase 'When you pray . . .' This is the third time he has said it and clearly he means to make clear two principles. Firstly in the new Kingdom there are to be no rules or regulations such as bound up the Pharisees. He laid down no guidance as to how often we should lay aside time to pray so we never are forced to pray by any legal requirement. We are free to pray as and when our circumstances and temperament require it. Our times may be regular or irregular – we are not to feel guilty about praying/not praying. God wants willing companions, not slaves. Secondly there will be times 'when we pray' if we are truly under the power of Jesus Christ. We shall no more be able to keep ourselves away from God than we can from any other person we really love. This one phrase sets us free to pray without bullying us into it.

Then look at the other assumption in the verse 'Your Father knows . . .'. If only we believed it then we actually would stop so much pointless 'babbling' both in private and public prayer. He hears our prayers and once we have truly set a matter before him, we need only to maintain it before him in total trust. He will act, He knows what we need, before we ask. It really is good to know that God is 'in the know' about all our circumstances, it certainly saves us from a lot of tedious explanations.

V.9 'This is how you should pray:' The same verse in Luke 11 v.2 reads, 'When you pray, say . . .'. Many of our difficulties in private prayer are rooted in an unrealistic expectation. We expect to be able to pray silently as the great saints and mystics have done. But Jesus said 'say' – formulate the words in your mind and express them with your lips. Speak out your private prayers. The very discipline of forming the words and phrases will help to make your prayer concrete. In time you will come to the place of silent prayer but you will *always* need to have private times of spoken prayer and praise. These are of immeasurable value in growing in prayer.

We must be clear that the prayer that follows was given as a pattern, not a formula to be slavishly repeated without thought. This therefore is the way Jesus recommends we arrange our prayer times:

(a) Relationships first

'**Our Father in heaven**'. We tend to rush in to the presence of God, bursting with our worries and problems. Jesus makes it crystal clear that we begin with relationships, two of them. We are related to the whole body of Christ and with them we are children of God. He is 'Our Father'. Furthermore he is not subject to the decay of our universe, he is 'in heaven', the eternal kingdom that never wears out and will last forever and ever. Because of this, he will *always* be 'Our Father'. His love for us will never die and will draw us on eternally into his heart.

(b) Worship

'**Hallowed be your name.**' Next Jesus brings us on to worship. Because of who God is and what he has made and above all what he has done, for us his name is to be special, loved and respected above all other names. Our reaction must be 'God, you are great, your name means so much to me'.

(c) Divine plans come true

V.10 **'Your Kingdom come, your will be done, on earth as it is in heaven'.** This for so many of us is the crunch point of prayer. What are we praying for? Is it to get God to do what we want? (God give me a Maserati/mansion in Sunningdale/the local beauty queen). Or do we pray to align ourselves with the will of God so that through us he begins to accomplish his purposes? Jesus made it clear we cannot even start to ask God about our needs, wants or desires until we have settled the matter of his total sovereignty. 'Your Kingdom come, your will be done'. These two phrases are actually in the form of royal commands. God originally appointed man to reign over the earth and so when we are born again and filled with his Spirit we are restored once again to that royal function. Here Jesus unveils the awesome power of prayer, it commands the blessing of God himself. He who longs to bless our fallen world, through our prayers of royal command unleashes his grace and power into the darkened planet. So these prayers are as big as our vision cares to make them. Only we cannot at the same time say 'my will be done' – these are prayers of real abandonment to God's royal authority and loving will. When we say 'on earth as it is in heaven' there are no limits – we give him all earth, including our bit of it and ourselves as part of it. This means that at times you will say this with tears and heartbreak. Keep faith with him, his will is always for our good in the end.

(d) Needs, Not Wants

V.11 **'Give us today our daily bread.'**

The first word most of us ever really pray is 'give' and how much we want him to give us! As Jesus made clear, God loves to give to his children – he loves to give good gifts. Notice there is a lot of difference between 'good gifts' and 'selfish demands'. He will give us the bread, that is the wholesome thing we need to sustain life, but because he is a loving Father, he will *not* give in to our spoilt pleadings for this indulgence or that luxury. What he gives to us comes as a loving gift not as the result of intensive negotiation by the 'Christian Family Trade Union'. By the way, it is never true that God does not hear or answer prayer – he does 'daily' and gives today what we need. His attention to us is constant.

(e) Forgiveness

V.12 **'Forgive us our debts, as we also have forgiven our debtors.'** What a terrifying lesson Jesus teaches here, and in verses 14–15. You will experience freedom from guilt only to the same extent as you release others from their guilt towards you. Retain their guilt in your heart, feed on resentment towards them and you cannot be forgiven. This applies no matter what their offence is, no matter how innocent you may be. Let us learn the lesson; we have sometimes such a prickly attitude to the world around. Let us be people who gladly, freely forgive all manner of offences against us, then we shall be truly free.

(f) Warfare

v.13(i) **'And lead us not into temptation, but deliver us from the evil one'.** Jesus teaches us to ask for two things in the light of the fact that Satan is the destroyer, longing to tear Christian believers to pieces. The first request is for clear guidance; guidance that God will lead us to avoid situations in which our weaknesses will lead to moral, spiritual or mental defeat and collapse. It is a request for wisdom and is bound to be granted provided only one condition is fulfilled: we must be prepared to obey the clear, sane guidance that God gives. The second request is simply for protection from the direct malice of the enemy. It is clear from the story of Job and the writings of Paul, to take just two examples, that Satan does attack Christians from time to time on the physical, psychological, mental, emotional and spiritual levels. We have joined the army of Jesus Christ and cannot expect to be exempt from our duties as soldiers of the king. We will be attacked, but the Lord is able to deliver us from the attacker. All he requires from us is the spirit that hangs on to him and even when all hope is gone says, like David 'my soul clings to thee'. In time, when his purpose for us is fulfilled and his power in us vindicated, he will bring us out from the attack and will give us the fierce joy of victory.

'I pursued my enemies and overtook them, I did not turn back till they were destroyed . . . You armed me with strength for the battle . . . You have delivered me . . . The Lord lives! Praise be to my Rock! Exalted be God my Saviour! (from Psalm 18 v.37–46 NIV)

(g) Adoration
V.13 (ii) 'For yours is the kingdom and the power and the glory, forever, Amen.'

Though these words are not in the earliest manuscripts and may not have been said at the time by Jesus, they are still very ancient. They fit so well on the end of the prayer, it is almost impossible to believe that they are not meant to be there. Like many, therefore, I believe them to be authentic, preserved in some other document and added in later manuscripts. This is the way to finish our private prayers with a time of adoration and praise of the one whose plans will come to pass, no matter how long it may seem to take. And he is glorious in majesty and beauty. To go out into an often drab and dreary world with this vision should make us like Moses, whose face shone as he emerged from the presence of the Lord.

Each of the seven sections of Jesus' outline for private prayer can take as little or as much time as we want to give. He does not lay upon us the burden of a minimum time limit. But if we use this pattern 'when we pray' we shall find a new wholesomeness in our relationship with him.

1. Relationship
2. Worship
3. Divine plans
4. Needs
5. Confession and forgiveness
6. Guidance and warfare
7. Adoration.

III PUBLIC PRAYER

So often the words 'Prayer Meeting' are the signal for a period of uncomfortable silence with occasional uninterested monologues given in mock-Elizabethan English. The embarrassment felt by most of us at such things is demonstrated by our absence from the proceedings.

It seems clear that the greatest problem is that we forget the main purpose of a prayer meeting is not that we should meet each other for a period of saying prayers. The purpose is that we together should meet God, recognising his power and presence in all creation and by prayer become agents of that presence and power. A prayer meeting is the specific God-designed means by which he releases his power into our world. Anything can happen through prayer because it engages the mighty hand of God, and that is truly exciting.

It is clear that the only way we can change our

attitudes so that public prayer is truly meeting God corporately is by the revival of our private prayer. People who have cultivated the habit of constant communion with the Lord Jesus, their heavenly lover, will not keep quiet when they meet him in public. Those who have set aside (regularly or irregularly) frequent times of deliberate prayer will not be lost for words in public. They have already trained themselves in the sevenfold pattern of Jesus.

Prayer meetings where such people meet are the most exciting events on the face of the earth. Through them the life of God is released into our dead world. Prayer of that kind will one day bring about the Apocalypse (Revelation). On that day God will answer the prayer 'Amen. Come Lord Jesus.' The curtain that hides heaven will be torn apart and on a highway of his people's prayer the king will return. 'Lord, teach us to pray.'

3: The Bible

It may be the oddest and at the same time the most scandalous factor in the spiritual weakness of the Church in the West – the strange anomaly that as we accumulate more and more translations of the Bible we actually read them less and less.

Of course some may wish to quarrel with the description of the Church as spiritually weak, pointing to growth in membership, larger budgets, extended buildings. Let me explain, none of these things necessarily mean growing *spiritual* strengh. That is demonstrated by increasing love, purity and integrity in the lives of God's people at personal, family, business and church level. It is also clearly shown by the power to resist temptation, overcome sin, triumph in suffering and confront organised evil in the world.

Just one nasty fact will serve to illustrate our increasing spiritual weakness: the horrifying acceleration in the divorce rates among 'committed Christian' families. As in most sociological effects the United States is 5-10 years ahead of Europe in terms of the *numbers* of Christian couples divorcing. But the trend on both sides of the Atlantic is in the same direction – upwards. What is worse, and truly frightening, is the increasing number of Christian 'leaders' who have abandoned biblical standards in this matter, not only wantonly divorcing but remarrying and continuing in highly public ministry.

We are not drawing attention to this in order to indulge in the 'shock horror' tactics of the gutter press, with its delighted sharing in others' sin. Nor can we stand in sanctimonious judgment over others. We are too aware of our own weakness and *must* affirm, 'There but for the grace of God *I* go.' The point of what we are saying is that Satan is attacking Christian homes and families as *never* before and he sees our weakness as his opportunity. It is reported that in England alone there are 1,000 Satanist groups actively interceding for the breakdown of the marriages of Christian *leaders*.

Against such a massive onslaught, what can we do? Who is sufficient for these things? Let us look at the Lord Jesus, freshly anointed with the power of the Holy Spirit and newly confirmed in his identity as the Son of God. Faced with Satanic temptation to satisfy personal, bodily and psychological desires, we see him resisting not by reference to his unlimited empowering or his divine identity but by the power of the written word of God. The divine Word himself gave his stamp to the written word by using it for his own protection. Furthermore, a careful textual examination of his teaching reveals scores of direct quotations and hundreds of allusions to the Old Testament writings. Jesus was a man of the Bible and was so intimately acquainted with it that its thought-forms came out quite unconsciously in his teaching. It was from this close involvement with the actual text of the Jewish Bible that he derived his spiritual endurance, moral power, and deep wisdom. If we want to be like him (if we do not there is something fatally wrong in our Christianity) then we must feed on the same food – 'you are what you eat'.

What is even more devastating than the rising divorce rate to which we have already referred is the fact that it is happening in areas of the world where there is more Bible teaching than ever before in history. Our weakness is not due to a lack of knowledge of Christian doctrine. It is primarily that we have ceased to personally interact with the text. We are a people of second-hand spirituality. We must once again become a people of one book, and that book the Bible.

Now this does not mean that we should have a superstitious attitude to the Bible. Some attribute an almost magical power to its words or even the pages on which it is printed. Such as attitude owes more to the influence of horror movies than to the example of the Lord Jesus and the great saints. Yet there are many Christians who have an overweening regard for the Scriptures, feeling that somehow just memorising and studying them conveys spiritual power. To such people the word of Jesus is clear: 'You diligently study the Scriptures because you think that by them you possess eternal life. These are the Scriptures that testify about me, yet you refuse to come to me to have life' (John5:39 NIV). The Scriptures do not exist for their own sake, they are to introduce us to Jesus Christ so that joined to him we may share his life.

One more warning. Through the centuries the people of God have been terribly vulnerable to the temptation of being 'right'. That is, convinced that we have understood correctly what the Bible says and having adjusted our lives accordingly we begin to congratulate ourselves on having got it all 'right'. Intellectual understanding becomes a substitute for the power of the spirit; this is a deadly danger producing the most hideous hyprocrisy. And a man in this position, because what he believes is right, may be totally unable to see how wrong he really is. The Pharisees were like this. Remember, only God is right. We must be people truly 'of a new covenant – not of the letter but of the Spirit; for the letter kills, but the Spirit gives life' (2 Cor. 3:6 NIV).

From Genesis to Revelation the Bible is first and foremost the revelation of the living God. God has revealed himself in the glories of nature, the mountaines and lakes, the great oceans and the inland seas, the coastal plains and the quiet hills and valleys, the hawk hovering high in the sky by the motorway, the bees that buzz in the heavy scented air of summer days, the great whales moving majestically and porpoises leaping playfully, the awesome power of the wind smashing mighty trees to matchwood. All this and much more is his way of declaring to man that he loves and delights in the teeming variety of his creation and in the infinitely varying personalities of men. But he knows that in a fallen world even such clear testimony will be misunderstood or ignored so he has revealed himself in the most remarkable book the world has ever seen.

In fact, the Bible is a small library carefully collected by men under the guidance of the Spirit of God so as to give a clear revelation of himself. It consists of 66 books written over a period of about 1,500 years by over 40 authors. As well as the time difference, just think of the enormous cultural and geographical divisions between the authors. Moses, carefully collating all the records of Abraham's family and recording the rigorously preserved stories of men in prehistory, almost certainly did most of his work in the wilderness wanderings. Paul lived in another world: the first century culture was one of confident new technologies, rapid sociological change, and of personal mobility undreamed-of before the Roman Empire. Yet they wrote of the same God and agreed about him. Again and again as you read the Bible you must be amazed by the realisation that they knew and loved the *same God*. There is no other explanation.

More than this, consider the enormous differences in personality types. The passionate and poetic young prophet Jeremiah burning in his love for God, breaking his heart over God's faithless people . . . Luke, the coolly analytical historian of the Early Church . . . Hosea, the prophet whose wife became a harlot, writing of God's pain as he seeks to win back his lost love, Israel . . . Amos, the rugged, stern herdsman, fearlessly warning a selfish, greedy society of judgment to come . . . Isaiah, the literary giant, whose colossal vision spanned world events and history . . . Ezekiel, the mystic, an aristocrat and political prisoner whose vivid imagination made his writing enormously powerful . . . John the fisherman, another mystic, who saw all time and history from eternity's perspective . . . James, the severely practical, no one ever called *him* a mystic. These men, so different, gave united testimony to the God of all peoples and all times.

The fascination of the Bible is endless once you understand that through its pages the living God is revealing himself. Just as the outlines of human personality are made known in interaction with others, so through his close involvement in the lives of his people he is painting an intimate portrait of his private face. However, it is not only in the fascinating interplay of the relationship between the great creator and the writers that we see revelation. What they wrote sprang out of that relationship. It dominated their lives and transformed their view of the world and its history. Knowing the God of all things, heavenly and earthly, in time and eternity, they saw him every-where they looked.

The Old Testament
The first part of the Bible, known to Christians as the Old Testament, is basically the Jewish Bible. More than 30 authors writing over about 900 years produced it.

The first part, Genesis to Esther, is the historical record. It begins with the creation story, not concentrating on how but on *why* God made all things. From the tragedy of the Fall it continues with the amazing narrative of his determination to fulfil his promise to Abraham that through the Jewish people, his family, all the people of the earth would be blessed.

The next section is usually called the 'Wisdom Literature'. These five books, from Job to the Song of Solomon contain some of the finest artistic writing the world has ever seen. The writers used poetry, drama and song to wrestle with the terrible contradictions of a supremely good, loving God and a horribly fallen creation, dominated by selfish, greedy, shallow and twisted people. One explored the cynical emptiness of life without God. Another produced the most beautiful exploration of romance and sexual significance that I have ever read.

The third section, 'The Prophets', runs from Isaiah to Malachi. In one case-history after another the passionate love of God for his rebellious people moves a prophet to stand before society, confronting it with its hypocrisy, selfishness and faithlessness. Increasingly, idolatry, cruelty and greed mark the chosen people of God, and terrifying warnings are spoken of judgment to come. Finally disaster, defeat and exile come, followed by the return of a remnant to the promised land.

In all this the writers were demonstrating that once you know God, who made all things and all people, you can see him at work in everything, in creation and fall, personal and national history, triumph and tragedy, rebellion and restoration. Their vision was enormous, reflecting the greatness of the God who had shown himself to them.

The New Testament

Five hundred years later the same vision gripped the writers of the New Testament. But the portrait of God so clearly implied and described by Old Testament writers was now clarified and finalised. The God of History had entered space-time himself to participate as a human in the unfolding story of his spoilt and perverted creation. He had experienced all it meant to live as a man in a fallen world. He had known rejection, loneliness, despair, tragedy and triumph. Now the glorious task of those who wrote was to record that the living God himself had become a man, lived a radiant life, died as love triumphant, rose again to liberate all men from guilt, failure and fear of death. Everything had changed.

So the New Testament also begins with history. The four Gospels give four different views of the man Jesus and see him in four different roles. Matthew, as a tax collector for the Romans had been a traitor to his Jewish heritage. Therefore, when he met Jesus and was restored to the God of Abraham, Isaac and Jacob, he met Jesus the Ultimate Jew. His story of Jesus is the story of the long-promised King, the Messiah, who in his coming and person fulfils at last the longings of God's covenant people. His is the face of a lion – the king.

Mark, however, writes as a young man who from his teenage years has been gripped by the dynamic expansion of the Early Church. He is held by the unbelievable adventure of the first disciples meeting the living God in their own kitchens. So the image that dominates his story is Christ the man of action; not the man of fake heroics but the man whose commitment to action made him a servant of all. Like the ox that lived in every Jewish home, ready to give its massive strength whenever needed, Mark's Jesus was a domestic God – at home with people.

When we come to Luke's story we have the approach of the trained investigator. Accustomed as a doctor to assembling data, he carefully placed Jesus in his historical context. More than that, he saw Jesus from the perspective of the Gentile world. He was a Greek and undoubtedly knew about the debate in the Grecian culture on 'the perfect man'. In Christ, at last, he saw him, the perfect human being, and rather than debate the topic he described the reality.

By the time John wrote his story some years after the other Gospels were completed, some members of the Early Church were questioning the divine origin of Jesus. John recognised that the need was for a record that would gather the evidence for the divinity of Christ. So, drawing on his experience as one of the twelve, he wrote the story of the Jesus he remembered. It is carefully constructed, not on a chronological basis, but from his intensely personal memories. Starting the story from the stand-point of eternity, 'In the beginning was the Word . . .', he finishes by confessing that the task was impossible. Jesus was just too rich and full of life to get down on paper. Yet he and they succeeded in doing just that. Time and again I have been gripped by the sheer reality of the story; like millions of others, I have met the living Jesus in the pages of the New Testament.

The history section of the New Testament finishes

with the book of Acts, which should perhaps be called: 'The Gospel of Jesus Christ according to Luke – Part II.' It is the continued story of the Lord and Christ of the Gospels now living in very ordinary, fallible men – the demonstration that once a group of people know the reality of Colossians 1, verse 27: 'Christ in you the hope of glory,' nothing is impossible to them. They become agents of divine power in the world of men.

The next section, from Romans through to Jude, is a collection of letters, some to churches and some to individuals. They cover almost every aspect of living and believing in Jesus Christ. Written in the first century of the Church age, they are still relevant today. Ringing with the excitement of men who were daily discovering more of Jesus Christ and beginning to realise just how great was the good news – spanning history from beginning to end and straddling the whole world.

The last book is the crown, not only of the New Testament but of the whole Bible. Firmly rooted in the historical records of both Testaments, John the author writes with total confidence, knowing the God who having proved himself in ancient and recent history can be trusted for the future. He draws freely on the rich imagery of the Psalms and weaves it together with the great future visions of the prophets. From the epistles (the letters) he takes the full-grown divine authority and eternal nature of Jesus Christ the Lord and Son of God, and shows him to us reigning in radiant glory co-equal with his Father. And in the last act of the great romance he places the most beautiful bride in history – the Church, splendid in heaven's loveliness 'having the glory of God' – next to her bride-groom to reign with him for ever and ever. It's the most exciting story ever told *and it is all true!*

Purpose of the Bible

Now the first purpose of the Bible is to reveal the living God – Father, Son and Holy Spirit – to men and women, so that seeing him they may enter into that relationship with him for which they were made. But the Bible is not only given to us for revelation of the nature, character and personality of God, it is given so that we may be on the inside of his plans. He wants us to know and participate in his purposes. The broad outline of Bible teaching gives to all of us a clear insight into the meaning and direction of history – we know where it is going and how it functions, we understand the underlying principles and the hidden factors at work in society. So the Bible is a practical book because it first provides us with a general direction and orientation within space and time. Like a compass needle swinging to North because its metallic particles come under the influence of magnetic forces, so the heart of a Christian is aligned with the purposes of God as the Holy Spirit works on the deposit of biblical truth within him.

But this works not only in a general sense: it is true also of specific guidance. Reading and studying the Bible attunes a Christian to God's voice and accustoms that same Christian to his speech patterns. That enables a man or woman to discern the true guidance of the Holy Spirit when confusion grips them. So the author of Psalm 119 says, 'Your word is a lamp to my feet and a light to my path' (v.105). Reading the Bible provides to the human mind and spirit God's own lighting system; for 'my feet' – what I should do; and 'my path' – what is happening around me.

The second aspect of the Bible's practical importance is its use as a versatile weapons system, embodying defence and attack capability. Many Christians seem to have forgotten that just being a Christian gives the Devil all the excuse he needs to let all Hell loose on them. They skip blithely through life naively imagining that because God has invaded their personality as promised, all must now go smoothly. Reality usually intervenes in the shape of vicious attacks by temptation, trouble or tragedy. In situations like this the Bible is invaluable; not only does it clearly detail the armour we all need every day of our lives (Eph. 6:10–17); it also provides us with the power to defend ourselves and fight back. We have already thought about the way the Lord Jesus countered the attacks of Satan (Luke 4:1–12) by using the Bible. In fact, he provides a perfect example of the biblical anti-missile missile!

When Satan used the Bible to tempt Jesus, he shot down the attack by using another Bible verse! Read, study and learn the Bible for your own survival.

Thirdly, the Bible is food for the Christian, providing all the essential nutritional requirements both for our growth and our daily sustenance. It has the food we need right from the beginning of our Christian lives: milk for the infant tummy (Heb. 5:12) and for the adult stomach (Heb. 5:14), and we should all long to grow up so that we can cope with adult food (1 Cor. 3:2). Some parts of the Bible are like a juicy steak, full of protein and succulent tastiness (e.g. Col. 1:15–20 and Eph. 3:14–21), but to live on these alone is unhealthy. Just as a healthy physical diet requires a balance of protein, carbohydrate, fibre, etc., so with the spiritual diet. And the Bible provides all these vital ingredients together with essential trace elements, i.e. small amounts of doctrines so powerful that only a tiny trace is enough for health: for instance, see what 1 John 3 v.2 and Revelation 22 v.5 imply about your future.

Fourthly, the Bible is a mirror; and because it is

undistorted and clear in itself it gives a clear image of whoever looks into it. So, regular Bible-reading provides to the person who is open to God's spirit a constant check on his state as a human being made to reflect the image of God. Anyone who can read the Bible complacently and untroubled is simply not seeing his own reflection; he is in dreadful danger.

If all these things are true, why do we not read the Bible as we should? The major factor for many of us is the 'TV factor'. Dominated by the television and film media, our all-pervasive entertainment industry feeds us with a constant diet of situations with instant, easy and constant excitement. Like the insistence on always being in the highly charged state known as 'being in love'. This is totally unrealistic. Life is not like that. And the Bible is true to life. It projects the high adventure of a man against all the powers of darkness and hell, and the cosmic romance of the kidnapped bride, the Church, awaiting rescue by her bridegroom-lover, against the background of ordinary everyday life. It does this because these mighty adventures are yours and mine. We who walk with Jesus Christ in this fallen world live out these epics in our daily lives. So the Bible is for *us*, to enable us to truly live by the power of the God who now indwells us.

Though some people have seen God as entirely outside his creation so that to them nature is a closed system and itself blindly sovereign, all the evidence is against them. They have often tried to tell the rest of us that there is no supernatural power and the Bible is only another book with many errors. However, all their attacks have only made clear how mighty the foundation of Bible truth really is. And all the research thus generated has clearly demonstrated that it is historically accurate and reliable in every way.

God has given us his truth in a book. I once picked up a record and the album sleeve said, 'You are holding a record of the greatest rock and roll band in the world. *Why aren't you playing it?*'

When you hold in your hand the Bible, you are holding what the British Coronation Service describes as, 'The most valuable thing this world affords. Here is wisdom. This is the Royal Law. These are the living oracles of God.'

Why aren't you reading it?

4: Humility

'I am well aware that I am the 'umblest person going,'
said Uriah Heep modestly; 'let the other be where he
may. Mother is likewise a very 'umble person. We
live in an 'umble abode, Master Copperfield, but have
much to be thankful for. My father's former calling
was 'umble. He was a sexton.'

'What is he now?' I asked.

'He is a partaker of glory at present, Master Copperfield,' said Uriah Heep. 'But we have much to be
thankful for. . . .

It is a popular misconception that humility is the
province of the weak. Charles Dickens' brilliant portrait of the snivelling Uriah Heep only encouraged it.
'Blessed are the meek!' Jesus proclaimed, and many
have jumped to the conclusion that meekness and
weakness are the same thing.

Because Jesus was humble and meek, he has been
portrayed by some contemporary film-makers as a
fragile, blond-haired figure, liable to be blown over
by any gust of wind. It is an odd image for an artisan
who worked as a carpenter and survived a Roman
flogging without collapsing. To have survived the
hardship and suffering of his life, he must have been
a man of strength, yet the opposite impression is
frequently given. It is tragic to observe the damage
that this over-romanticised portrait has done, making

the Christian faith seem irrelevant to the working man.

. Dick Emery's caricature of the buck-toothed, eccentric vicar has contributed to the myth of the Christian as both weak-willed and wet! This impression of the Christian as a rather odd character who needs a crutch to survive has done much to damage the credibility of the Christian faith. It has also, unfortunately, pressured many of us into unconsciously going along with what the world expects. We see ourselves as those who must always give way, retreat, and become a pushover in the community. Instead of commending our deep humility this attitude simple confirms the suspicion that a Christian is 'a bit of a drip!'

It is true that the gospel calls us to a life of humility, but that requires strength rather than weakness. Humility involves willingness to be a servant, to stand alongside the downtrodden and oppressed, to seek to further the hopes and aspirations of others, to be more concerned for the needs of our neighbours than for ourselves, to forgive when forgiveness seems unthinkable. Such attitudes are hallmarks of the humble – and the strong!

He escaped assassination. His wife was wounded saving his life. His only son was murdered. His fellow priests were killed, imprisoned, or forced into exile. Friends and colleagues, including his Secretary, Jean Waddell, and John and Audrey Coleman, were imprisoned, accused of spying.

How does an ordinary man suffer and forgive at one and the same time? H. B. Dehqari-Tafti, the Bishop of Iran, wrote his personal testimony to the strength which God gives to those humble enough to acknowledge their own weaknesses. 'The power to suffer hardship, persecution, and martyrdom was granted to us by God for each event as it happened, one after another, and we thank him for counting us worthy to witness to his love.'[1]

Nowhere in the gospel do we discover a mandate to fight to become spiritual superstars who ask to be looked up to by everybody. Nor do we find justification for the feeble, nervous, weak-willed retreat of a spiritual 'wet'. To live a life which is not self-centred does not require weakness but strength; because such a life-style is swimming against the tide and refusing to conform to the norms of our society. Weakness is illustrated when, like cattle, we blindly follow the herd. The strength of the Christian is seen when we take a stand and demonstrate the fact that we are different! This must never only be seen in a negative context by what we *don't* do, but rather by the positive actions we take to serve and care for each other, and indeed for society as a whole.

The Kingdom of God employs principles which are exactly the opposite to those which society would expect. Jesus called his people to be holy, and the Greek word employed there (hagios, ´dyios) means to be 'different'. Servanthood and gentleness in character are seen by the world as marks of failure, but Jesus announced exactly the opposite!

When his disciples competed among themselves as to who would be the greatest in the Kingdom, Jesus did not point to natural ability or self-confidence, but used these words, 'You know that the men who are considered rulers of the heathen have power over them, and the leaders have complete authority. This, however, is not the way it is among you. If one of you wants to be great, he must be the servant of the rest; and if one of you wants to be first, he must be the slave of all' (Mark 10 vv 42–44 GNB).

Pulpits can be difficult things!

The preacher can be too far from the congregation. He can be raised supposedly above the level of contradiction. A pulpit can also contain hidden messages secretly sellotaped to the lectern. One such message demanded, 'Sir, we would see Jesus.' What a demand, what pressure on the preacher; I was stunned at the request. It conjured up the idea that somehow I had to produce the goods!

In John 12 this demand was made of Philip by a bunch of Greeks. They were looking for another spiritual experience to prop them up and were presumably not far away from the present-day congregation asking to see Jesus. The desire to be spectators wandering from one spiritual highlight to the next is strong in the Church today. Jesus refused to grant the request. Instead he suggested that rather than wanting to see we should want to serve. We will never truly encounter the living God by standing on the sidelines observing the action. We must get fully involved in his service.

The question must never be, 'How can we see Jesus?' All that desire can ever produce is a continuation of the kind of spiritual spectator who fills our churches today. For many of us it is sufficient to sing the hymns, say the prayers, listen to the sermons, but avoid the action! We think such things will draw us closer to the Lord, but his demands are far more fundamental:

'Truly, truly, I say to you, unless a grain of wheat falls into the earth and dies, it remains alone; but if it dies, it bears much fruit . . . If any one serves me, he must follow me; and where I am, there shall my servant be' (John 12:24–26 RSV). Strangely enough, in serving Jesus we discover our need to receive more from him. We can be drawn closer and closer because we are involved in his service.

Such teaching is far from normal today. We are often told that God wants some vague ethereal tribute of worship but is not interested in our actions. That is nonsense. There can be little hope for a fellowship which stresses either worship or service alone because they should be indissolubly linked.

Loving Jesus for all
that he is and does

Seeing what he
does as a result
of our service

Worshipping him
Expressing
our love

Service
Sharing his love
with others

Out of our love for Jesus should flow worship, and our worship should lead to service, which must result in deeper love and worship; and so the process continues growing as it is repeated!

The Bible launched the concept of two Kingdoms: two ways of life, one which acknowledged the rule and authority of God in the life of the individual, and the other which demanded the right to 'do my own thing.' In the kingdom of man the struggle is to get all that we can for ourselves. The Kingdom of God was intended to demonstrate a radically different life-style in which humility and servanthood replaced arrogant self-interest.

Jesus lived a life totally given over to the needs of others. He fed the hungry, healed the sick and told of a new life which God and man would share together. Instead of spending all his time with the religious and elite Jesus mixed with 'untouchables' and finally died a brutal death out of compassion for men and women trapped in the vicious cycle of sin and death.

Imagine the astonishment of the disciples when the one they had begun to recognise as the Son of God took on the role of the most insignificant servant in the household. 'He poured some water into a basin and began to wash the disciples' feet and dry them with the towel' (John 13:5 GNB).

Recently, a friend of mine performed exactly the same action in an East End church, telling the church members that this was a practice which he had learned from his closest friend! Whether or not we perform this specific act, Jesus intended that we should learn a very basic lesson, a lesson which would, if lived out in our society, demonstrate that the Kingdom of God is not merely a future event. It is here and now.

Jesus intended that his Kingdom should invade the kingdom of this world. To achieve that purpose his would be an army of servants, a people who would shake their society to its foundations. Instead of looking after themselves they would give their lives in service to others. By so doing they would vividly demonstrate that they knew the living God and that he reigned as King among them.

'We love because God first loved us. If some one

says he loves God, but hates his brother, he is a liar. For he cannot love God, whom he has not seen, if he does not love his brother, whom he has seen. The command that Christ has given us is this: whoever loves God must love his brother also' (1 John 4:19–21). It was this miracle of reorientation, from love of self to love of others, which in an amazing way marked out the Early Church as a different kind of people. So much so that the historian, Tertullian, proudly recorded the gossip of several pagans who commented in amazement, 'See how these Christians love one another!'

Listen

A servant will hear his master's voice. If we are to serve God then we must hear what he says to us, however basic the instruction may be.

Last year, as always, I took my family with me to Spring Harvest, Youth for Christ's annual teaching for evangelism conference. Now my wife and I have three children all under seven years old. The children know that daddy is either away, 'talking to people about Jesus,' or at home with them. They therefore find Spring Harvest a difficult time. Daddy is with them and yet keeps going off to lead a seminar or share in the organisation of the events.

In an attempt to make up for this it has become family policy that directly after Spring Harvest we go away together just to escape for a few days. On this occasion we stayed for two nights at an hotel in Llangollen and had a tremendously relaxing time. When we set off for home my wife anxiously enquired if we could afford it. The bill had come to £75 and the frank answer would have been 'No', but I tried to reassure her because we had little option and it had been worth every penny.

I was concerned but went off the next day to conduct a clergy breakfast for a local Youth for Christ centre. Imagine my surprise when, having never even mentioned money, a local businessman came up afterwards and said, 'I enjoyed the meeting, but while you were speaking the Lord told me to give you this and said that you would know what it was for.' The cheque was for exactly £75. Now that is an unusual amount, but the man who listened to God knew how to act on what God told him! Some months later I was speaking at a series of meetings and felt it right to tell this story, while keeping the businessman's identity anonymous. Later I discovered that he had been in the meeting and was very encouraged.

It is good to recognise that our Lord Jesus is the Creator God who has our lives in his hand and longs to order them in his own way. If we listen to his voice, and do what he tells us, who can guess the blessing it brings? My wife, family and I will always be grateful for that businessman. He, along with so many others, has learned the lesson which God is teaching us. In the words of Mary, 'Do whatever he tells you!' (John 2:5).

Care!

'I was hungry but you would not feed me, thirsty but you would not give me a drink; I was a stranger but you would not welcome me in your homes, naked but you would not clothe me; I was sick and in prison but you would not take care of me.' Then they will answer him, 'When, Lord, did we?' . . . The King will reply, 'I tell you, whenever you refused to help one of these least important ones, you refused to help me' (Matt. 25:42–45).

Recently my family and I flew off from Gatwick Airport on holiday. We were driven to the airport in the early morning by a local Christian leader. He took my car back to his home (saving a small fortune in airport car parking) and then met us all on our return. This simple act of service was performed by a Christian leader whom I had never met before.

How much do we need to recover that kind of humility which is not content with self-effacement? Jesus is not looking for 'shrinking violets' hiding in a corner, but for those who will actively demonstrate their love and care for others. Jesus himself was highly visible in all he said and did, but all his activities were directed towards helping his neighbours.

I am often absent-minded, particularly after preaching! One friend is a notable Christian composer, arranger and musician. To my way of thinking his abilities are surpassed by the way that, time and again, he searches the stage after a concert or presentation. Often he discovers that I have left my Bible behind and comes running after me to return it. A few minutes before, hundreds have been applauding his abilities but he can only see himself as a servant of Christ trying to help others in the simplest way available to him.

I know several men and women like that. They actively care for the needs of others with a deeper concern than they have for themselves.

Hurt!

Our family comprises one girl and two boys. At one stage of his life, the youngest, Gavin, fell over three times in a month. The last time he gashed his lip and was taken to hospital for three stitches. He was screaming at his own hurt, but his brother and sister were hurting for him; they longed to do something to make him feel better.

We all face trouble and difficulties; from time to

time things get on top of us. One of the greatest joys of real Christianity lies in learning how to feel with the needs and hurts of others. Self-interest has dominated for too long. Society sits up and starts to take notice when it sees people more concerned for the welfare of others than for themselves.

The comments of the apostle Paul to the Roman Church were quite straight-forward: 'Open your homes to strangers. Ask God to bless those who persecute you . . . Be happy with those who are happy, weep with those who weep. Have the same concern for everyone' (Rom. 12:13–16).

I wonder if you have a car? Do you have a sticker on the rear window.

I used to do a lot of hitch-hiking in pre-Christian days. I grew very used to seeing texts: they were on the rear of cars going past me! Only one car with a text ever stopped and I gained a very distinct impression of an unfeeling Christianity.

A friend of mine was driving home one Sunday evening. A young man was sitting in the road making his final protest against society. She half dragged him into the car and took him home. She and her husband gave him food, a bed and helped him find a job. It's not surprising that he was so impressed with their concern that he began asking questions. They led him to Jesus and took him to their church. Seven years later he is a leader in the church, married to a Christian girl, and really going on with God. All because a Christian woman felt his hurt and stopped to give positive help!

The unfeeling and uncaring attitude which leads us to ignore so many human needs makes a travesty of all the claims of Jesus. We should have a name as the people who feel the hurts of our world and seek to meet those needs with the love and compassion of Jesus.

How dare we drive past someone standing by the roadside, cold and dripping wet in the pouring rain while our text boldly proclaims, 'Jesus loves you.' As Krishna so pertinently remarked, after examining the lives of Christians for many years, 'Christians claim that Jesus Christ is the Saviour of sinners, but they show no more signs of being saved than anyone else.'

Being humble means overturning the standards of the world by feeling more for the needs of others than our own.

Share!

One thing that can amaze non-Christians is the way in which reserved, inhibited Englishmen are learning to spontaneously demonstrate their loving concern for one another. I was in Ayr, Scotland, staying with friends, when at 2.15 am the telephone rang and I learned that my father had died. Dave Pope came into the room, quietly put his arm around me and just stayed. Meanwhile, John Daniels warmed up his car and drove me through the night to Lancaster, while another friend stepped into his car in Birmingham and drove to Lancaster to meet me there. He drove me on to meet my own car in Birmingham.

I'm an only child, and my mother was alone in Bexley, Kent. The neighbours sympathised with her after the funeral and one commented, 'Your son got to you quickly. 10.15 wasn't it? He couldn't have been far away?' When the neighbour heard that I'd been in Ayr and that friends had done so much to help, my mother had to explain that loving Jesus involves practical outgoing care. The neighbour was amazed, and rather thoughtful.

Our service towards each other and our relationship

together provide the most vivid possible demonstration that the Kingdom of God is being lived out amongst ordinary men and women in Britain today.

By sharing our homes, cars and material possessions we are only obeying Jesus' own commands and copying the practise of the Early Church. So fundamental was this commitment that Luke records, 'There was no one in the group who was in need' (Acts 4:34). Jesus prayed that his disciples might be 'completely one, in order that the world may know that you sent me and that you love them as you love me' (John 17:23). By our actions we can give a more positive expression of the gospel than our words can ever convey!

Help!

We can't divorce the proclamation of the gospel from a deep, caring commitment for people as people. A number of American churches have become involved in improving housing conditions. A house would be bought in a deteriorating area, renovated by the church members, and then offered for sale at a price that was within the means of lower income families. Of course, this project could never work without the freely given time and labour of church members who saw Christianity as far more than an endless procession of meetings. One of them commented, 'We are not just concerned about housing, we want to see people come to Christ.

And personally, I see no contradiction between kneeling down in prayer with a man as I lead him to Christ, which I've done many times, and kneeling down to nail linoleum on the floor so he can have a decent house to live in! It is just that combination of words and deeds which makes the gospel ring true! The work of Frontier Youth Trust with 'unclubable' teenagers; of In Contact with immigrant communities; and of British Youth for Christ with the unemployed are all illustrations of Christian caring attitudes paving the way for in-depth evangelism.

The life of servant-hood must never be just confined to our fellow Christians. A haughty, arrogant, 'better than thou' attitude towards the world in general has created a major barrier for far too long. It is possible for many moral, generous, concerned non-Christians to look at the Church and be nauseated by our insular attitudes. They see us as totally concerned with our meetings, our lives, and our friends. We seem to have little time for the humility of Jesus who unceasingly gave himself to others.

If we are to be a humble people then our humility cannot be confined to merely serving each other. We need to serve people because we share a common humanity with them and copy the example of the Son of Man who didn't come to judge mankind but to love, serve and bring them to his Father. 'If anyone hears my message and does not obey it, I will not judge him. I came, not to judge the world, but to save it.' 'I have not come to call the respectable people, but outcasts' (John 12:47; Mark 2:17).

It has often been pointed out that it is no good boldly proclaiming that 'Jesus is the answer' until someone is asking the question. It's not until our love and caring has been felt that people will start asking about our message.

Such service is not a weak, timid thing but a bold, outgoing concern which others have called 'tough love'.

At the US Congress on Evangelism in September 1969 one of the speakers humorously commented: 'Evangelism and social action have been like the old steamboat: when it whistled it couldn't move and when it moved it couldn't whistle.'[2]

Social concern is not merely offering help, it is an attitude which can receive as well as give. An American student went from a lifetime in Manhattan to the Dominican Republic as an agricultural missionary. He had no idea what he was doing, but he knew that God had called him to go. After about a fortnight the Spanish speaking Dominican farmers had pity on him and would go over to help him, after farming their own fields. Dave had one skill the local people lacked – he could read. Some of the local farmers had books in Spanish on improved farming techniques. Every night Dave would mouth the words; the farmers understood, and put into practice what they learned. Within eighteen months the agricultural productivity of that region increased by three hundred per cent. Dave went with no power, no knowledge, only love for the poor and the helpless.

'Service is not evangelism. Men, whatever their social class, economic condition or political position, need to know that God loves them and that Christ offers them the way to return to God . . . To proclaim the good news by preaching, personal testimony, literature and Bible distribution is always necessary, here and now, by every believer. But he who evangelises has a different life. He is someone who has learned to serve. He is a living letter which shows forth the truth and application of the message he proclaims. We can never separate the proclamation of the gospel from the demonstration of that gospel. They are different but both are indispensable.'[3]

Get down!

The advertising hoardings demand that we emphasise our own self-improvement:

'Better yourself'

'Keep up with the Joneses.'

'Get on.'

Sociologists call it 'upward mobility'. Christians often seem to struggle for the same objectives but in so doing they deny the character of Jesus.

He, alone, could choose where he was born, how he should live, what standards and comfort he could expect. Instead of choosing a palace, the Lord of Glory selected a stable. Instead of looking for influential parents, he joined the family of an artisan. Instead of a life of ease, Jesus knew the rigours of manual labour. Instead of mixing with the intelligentsia, he chose the company of sinners.

This deliberate plunge of the Lord of Glory into the lowest which humanity had to offer was to bring the salvation of the world. Christ's incarnation illustrates what he can expect from us:

Jesus obeyed his Father.

He gave himself to outcasts.

He endured rejection.

He refused the claims of personal ambition.

He lived in poverty.

He made the poor his people.

He lived a life for others.

So must we.

'To live in radical obedience to Jesus Christ means to be identified with the poor and oppressed. If that is not clear in the New Testament, then nothing is. God entered the human situation as one of the poor and powerless.'[4]

In no way did Jesus show any attitude of personal

superiority. His very humility enabled these people to feel secure with him.

'The poor, the defenseless, the weak, the sick, the vulnerable came to him because they had nowhere else to go. They became his people. He was sent to them to champion their cause, to comfort their spirits, to share their lives, to love them, to be with them. He refused to exercise power and control over them but came among them as a servant. When they tried to make him their king, he withdrew to the hills to pray. Instead, he would simply serve them, show them God's love for them, and ultimately give up his life on their behalf . . . If the poor were Christ's people and we are his body, then the poor became our people. If Christ was the servant of the poor, then, among the poor, the church lives as a servant people.'[4]

From his obscure birth in a dirty animal stable to his crucifixion on a Jerusalem rubbish dump Jesus demonstrated the gospel call to a downward pilgrimage.

One Anglican vicar recently commented to the effect that commitment to Christ brings us to a direct acceptance of middle-class values. However, the gospel presents a suffering sovereign who was content to live as the servant of the poor.

The basics of humility lie far away from the snivelling, cringing, Uriah Heep. By finding a life in which we listen, care, hurt, share, help and get down to the needs of our neighbours, we rediscover a truly biblical life-style. As Jesus said 'Take my yoke and put it on you, and learn from me, because I am gentle and humble in spirit; and you will find rest' (Matt. 11:29).

This gospel calls us to a life of humility which requires strength not weakness. Humility is an essential of servant-hood; to stand alongside the downtrodden and oppressed, to seek to further the hopes and aspirations of others, to be more concerned for the needs of our neighbours rather than ourselves.

To be humble will never be easy. I know in my own life how many times I react exactly the opposite way. As John Wesley once put it, 'It is difficult to be humble. Even if you aim at humility, there is no guarantee that when you have attained the state you will not be proud of the fact.' Yet for some people years of serving others has led to them seeing their own value in very clear perspective, without pride.

Thirteen years ago I was the editor of the student magazine at theological college. A visiting evangelist agreed to an interview. Due to meet the wife of an ex-President of the USA at Heathrow Airport, he insisted on giving time to the interview, an interview which led to an open sharing of all that God was doing worldwide. I sat spellbound as I listened to the man who, that afternoon, God used to call me into full-time evangelism. If humility involves thinking of others then he must rank as one of the humblest men I know. His public image was very different but I'll never stop being grateful for the way in which he gave of his time and himself to a young, insignificant student! His name – Billy Graham.

As Paul writes, 'Don't do anything from selfish ambition or from a cheap desire to boast, but be humble towards one another, always considering others better than yourselves. And look out for one another's interests, not just for your own' (Phil. 2:3–4).

5: Giving

Whether it's Abba or the Beatles, the Jam or the Pretenders, the cry has always been the same. From 'Give me money . . . that's what I want', to 'Money, Money, Money . . . it's a rich man's world.' Man's kingdom has always been founded on material possessions.

Our vocabulary reveals our preoccupation. Money, bread, loot, dough, notes, green or brass – the word varies but the thought remains the same. Whether my ambition is status, women, position or happiness, the route to all is seen to lie via the money road:

I've got a pocket full of pretty green –
I'm gonna put it in the fruit machine . . .

This is the pretty green – this is society –
You can't do nothing unless it's in the pocket . . .

I've got a pocket full of pretty green –
I'm gonna give it to the man behind the counter –
He's gonna give me food and water –
I'm gonna eat that and look for more –

And they didn't teach me that in school –
It's something that I learnt on my own –
That power is measured by the pound or the fist
It's as clear as this oh. . . .

This is the pretty green – this is society –
You can't do nothing unless it's in the pocket.

The Jam[1]

And still we never seem to have enough. Our demands are incessant. More and more for less and less. Sales, reduced prices, bargains, strikes, wage increases, inflation; these are the news-making words of today. The kingdom of this world is marked out by the struggle for bigger, better, newer, at every level. The car, the house, the stereo, the video; all these are seen as the status symbols on which to base our security.

Advertising agencies are not slow to promote this national syndrome. We are constantly encouraged to buy something better. Manufacturers treat built-in obsolescence (ensuring that their product will only remain fashionable or workable for a limited period of time) as a fact of life. Gone are the days when a product was bought to last a lifetime! The assumption is always that the consumer will require something new – with all the most fashionable refinements, of course!

We live in an age of consumerism. Banking and finance companies are geared to distribute capital so that we can buy now and pay later. Individual value is measured by the ability to purchase bigger, newer and better things. In a recent survey, opinion pollsters in Iowa have been asking which of the Ten Commandments people would eliminate if they had to. About 10 per cent chose the one about coveting their neighbours' goods, 4 per cent the injunction against adultery and 2 per cent the one about lusting after the neighbour's wife. 'In a recession,' said the analyst in the Des Moines Register, 'it showed a ridiculous bias towards business rather than sex!'

Sadly, the popular mind, and that of many Christians too, views the message of Jesus as having little to offer that is relevant to society today. Jesus' words, 'Well, then, pay the Emperor what belongs to the Emperor, and pay God what belongs to God' (Luke 20:25), are taken as a licence to live exactly as we wish on material issues, providing we give God spiritual worship. The exact nature of this worship is somewhat uncertain, but we do understand that the Lord has little desire to be involved in our practical material living!

Recently my wife, Ruth, and I were shopping in John Lewis at Milton Keynes. The store was pretty full because it was the first day of their annual sale. We had seen a hi-fi system which we had been trying to find for many months. It was reduced to a fairly ridiculous level. So we left the shop and prayed as we did the rest of our shopping elsewhere. We then returned to see if it was still there, which it was! So we stood over this hi-fi and quietly prayed. We knew that the Lord would have to provide the money and we didn't want anything in our home which he didn't want us to have. It seemed so natural just whispering together to the Lord. When we finished Ruth laughed, 'Look at everyone watching us!' No one could understand that we wanted to involve the living God in making a material purchase!

The other view which many hold is that God views all material involvement with a somewhat disapproving gaze, that he wants his people to be poor. How often does a church look to its minister and his family for a lead in humility and simple life-style with the helpful offer, 'God will keep him humble and we'll keep him poor!' From this stand-point Christianity is seen as being totally against technological advance and social improvement. It is regarded as having little to offer on such subjects as unemployment, labour relations, investment, bad housing, business, investment or poverty. The Christian attitude to cash is popularly misrepresented as, 'Money is the root of all evil.'

Contrary to public opinion, Jesus never spoke like that. His life-style vividly showed his lack of concern for material wealth. After all, he never charged anything for his services! Yet the disciples did have a treasurer, and presumably used money to meet their daily needs. Jesus did not spurn money, but he did display the concern that *the love of* money is the root of all evil.' Selfishness and greed were unsparingly condemned. Wealth which was not controlled by the Spirit of God was seen as a major barrier to entering the Kingdom. It was the accumulation and love of money and material prosperity which Jesus recognised as being so dangerous and, rather than ignore the subject, no less than 20 per cent of the verses in the Gospels concern Jesus' attitudes to material possessions.

The fact is that the gospel has much to say to many areas of our lives about which, quite honestly, we would far rather it were silent! Christianity is a very material faith. So much is based in the practical expressions of our daily lives.

In fact, Jesus' attitude was such that he pioneered a view of economics within the Kingdom of God which visibly demonstrated, in six specific areas, a radically alternative society. It was a society composed of ordinary people who would live their lives in the way which Jesus intended, and would clearly show the rest of society what loving and serving God truly involves.

Poverty

Jesus lived his whole life in relative poverty. He could have exploited his position for great personal gain. Instead, when he needed transport he had to borrow a donkey. To pay taxes Jesus arranged for a fish to provide the money! To make a point he had to borrow a coin, and the only legacy left after his death was his coat and that went to the soldiers who were killing him.

He left a carpenter's workshop and went on the road with no appeal for financial help. He recruited a band of followers with no offer of wages in material kind. Jesus' whole attitude was summarised in the Sermon on the Mount. 'Do not store up riches for yourselves here on earth, where moths and rust destroy, and robbers break in and steal. Instead, store up riches for yourselves in heaven, where moths and rust cannot destroy and robbers cannot break in and steal. For your heart will always be where your riches are' (Matt. 6:19–21).

Jesus is not exalting poverty, because God has specifically stated that he is against a society where poverty is tolerated. He told Israel that 'Not one of your people will be poor' (Deut. 15:4). This was given in terms of a command rather than a prophecy! Any economic system which bolsters the rich and oppresses the poor will never be condoned by the living God. He is specifically against any economic structure which fails to give equality of opportunity and restoration to every man. Israel was commanded to redistribute her wealth every fifty years. The year of Jubilee was simply the time when everyone reverted to the landholding which they had possessed fifty years before and started again! In that way no family could retain an undue prosperity and landholding in the community for longer than fifty years. God never wanted a situation which a friend of mine recently encountered on a visit to India. A man was begging because he had no arms. She was told that he had probably had his arms voluntarily amputated so that he could earn an adequate livelihood by begging. The presence of poverty is never a mark of the will of God, but of the fallen nature of man where greed and oppression are motivated by Satan himself.

What then does Jesus mean? He is not asking us, of necessity, to live in poverty. By saying, 'Your heart will always be where your riches are,' he is expressing the fact that there are alternative motivations in life. The life-style of the kingdom of the world demands that our heart is set on material things, but the life-style of the Kingdom of God demands that we see things very differently. Jesus sees earthly and heavenly fortune-hunting to be irreconcilable. We might want it to be a case of both/and; Jesus says it must be either/or for we can't serve God and material possessions. We must set our hearts on either one or the other.

In reality, as John White has put it, Jesus is not so much giving an instruction as an appeal to common-sense. He is not just making an arbitrary demand but a guide to life which will produce an end result.

'Clearly if earthly treasures are computable and insecure, we will do better to employ our time securing heavenly treasure. To transpose the recommended action to the twentieth century, if televisions go on the blink, cars depreciate, fashionable clothes go out of date, if bonds and jewels can be stolen, insurance companies go bankrupt, banks fail, and war and inflation destroy property and the value of money, it would make more sense to devote our energies to accumulating a celestial fortune.'[2]

Corruption

Is money wrong for a Christian? Should we save, take a mortgage, etc.? Here again the Scriptures are quite plain. 'If you work hard, you will get a fortune' (Prov. 12:27). 'A good man will have wealth to leave to his grandchildren' (Prov. 13:22). The wealth is not wrong in itself, but we must look at what it does to our hearts. How do we view money, how important does it become to us?

Christianity emerged within agriculturally orientated Palestine. The Bible is full of stories of sheep and donkeys, sermons delivered about harvests and vineyards, and several of the disciples were fishermen. What guidelines, if any, is it able to give towards coping with the economic concerns of our modern industrial society?

Three questions are raised.

1. *Relevance?* History has shown that a change in man's social order or economic standing has failed to change his human nature. There are greater economic differences (and inequities!) within today's world than there are between the economics of first century Jerusalem and twentieth century New York City. Within twenty-four hours I could leave the business world of the City of London and be in the middle of tropical jungles inhabited by Indians whose only means of livelihood consists of hunting, fishing and a few hand-planted crops. The relevance of the Christian message is not determined by either a time-period or a standard of economic development. The gospel is relevant to our industrialised society because the nature of man remains the same.

Jesus strongly emphasised the relationship between economics and man's personal relationship with God. For he declared, to a man whose blackmail and extortion was self-confessed, that 'Salvation has come to this house today' (Luke 19:9), only when Zacchaeus had first promised to make proper restitution to everybody he had cheated.

If attitudes towards possessions and the desire for material security were important then, how much more are they crucial now? The deceptive worship of materialism is a far more relevant obstacle to man's salvation today than it ever was in the first century.

The world says fight for all you can get. Jesus offered a totally different perspective and a completely radical alternative. He told his disciples not to be afraid of material things. Instead we were to seek for his Kingdom, then everything else would follow. When we pursue Jesus rather than money, our whole lives will be cared for by him.

2. *Allegiance*? Jesus' own words spelt out the problem. 'Look at the birds flying around: they do not sow seeds, gather a harvest and put it in barns; yet your Father in heaven takes care of them . . . So do not start worrying: "Where will my food come from? or my drink? or my clothes?" (These are the things the pagans are always concerned about.)' (Matt. 6:26,31–32). We cannot claim to serve God while we devote all our time and energy to materialistic self-interests.

Nowhere does Christ advocate the idea that a life of faith involves us all going through a series of set processes. We were not made to all function on the same economic level, but we *were* designed to operate at the level of the same economic obedience. Therefore, when a friend of mine and his wife share that God is calling them to sell their home and move into a much less affluent area, they are not demanding that I obey the same instruction. That was God's command to them. But the challenge is there to demonstrate the same attitude to material possessions. They are gifts given by God – just as he gives so he can demand in return!

The rich, young ruler is a classic illustration of a man stunned by the enormity of Jesus' request. Sell all he had? Why? Had not God given all this wealth? What sense was there in giving it up? Could it not be used well? Notably he did not argue with Jesus. He sensed that the demand was completely within Jesus' authority. He turned his back on Jesus, not in disgust, but in sadness. He knew too well the attractiveness of wealth and realised too late his allegiance to it.

3. *Possessions*? The living God gives gifts to us as his children. To some of us is given material wealth. The danger lies in the fact that, within our acquisitive society which places such undue emphasis on personal prosperity, these things can turn our hearts away from God and towards 'things'. TV sets, cars, houses, etc. can so easily take the place of God as King in our hearts.

Jesus ate, drank, and was clothed in such a way as not to draw undue attention to his poverty. Luke comments that Joanna and Susanna amongst others financially supported Jesus and the twelve disciples (Luke 8:3). Material possessions are not intrinsically evil. The problem lies between our grasp of them for our own self-gratification, or our desire to acquire and use what God gives us as faithful stewards of that which he has entrusted to us. The difference is between the spirit of greedy accumulation which characterises so many in the West and that which faithfully shares with others as God reveals the need.

The desire to care only for ourselves and our families is so strong, but such individualism is a curse. Its bloody logic has justified massacre and poverty worldwide. The 'I'm all right, Jack' syndrome affects Christian and non-Christian alike. So we stand by while others suffer, be those sufferings physical or economic. This moral cowardice stems from a failure to believe that God has provided for us in order that he might provide for others through us and then demonstrate his love by providing for us again.

A young couple met each other at York University. He was studying German and her degree course was in maths. They fell in love and on completing their courses they married. They gained teaching positions in a Midlands town, went to a local church, bought a house which they furnished from what money they had and a super range of wedding presents.

Financially, they were well off and they started a youth work with many of the kids from the school. A mission was planned for the school and a young evangelist stayed with them as part of the mission team. The mission went well and a few months later the evangelist was asked if he could drop in to see the couple.

When he did he was told that this young couple, who had not been able to have children, felt a clear call of God to go to West Africa to work with Wycliffe Bible Translators. They were therefore intending to leave the area to go to Bible College for further training before going on the mission-field. Their main problem was the house, furniture and wedding presents. They were certain that, despite being advised by well-meaning friends to sell their property and hold the money against a rainy day, the Lord was calling them to give away their house, furniture and wedding presents to the young evangelist and his wife.

Now this evangelist had earned the grand sum of £119, plus a few personal gifts, in his first year of ministry. He had then married, and the Lord had provided half a house, rent-free in the middle of London, given by a non-Christian who neither he, nor his wife, had ever met in their lives! This gift was for one year and the year was almost complete. The evangelist was quite speechless, totally amazed!

The local church couldn't believe it either and this demonstration of Christian obedience from the young couple did much to challenge many to a deeper commitment of their material possessions to Jesus. However, one set of parents was naturally disturbed. A week before the couple went to Bible College they had nowhere to live for their course of study. Imagine the amazement of the parents when they later visited them. The Lord gave them, for eight pounds a week, a country cottage with a swimming pool and tennis courts adjacent and available to them!

It is now ten years later. The couple now have two fine children and a great record of service for God. The evangelist and his wife who faced no home and no furniture were provided for life with a total gift which left only the remains of the mortgage to pay (and a Christian Bank Manager helped to arrange that!). They also knew that they served a God who loved, cared and provided for their personal needs through his people.

I know of several such incidents. This one I know in detail. I should – I was the young evangelist. Everything my wife and I have we owe to two people who listened to Jesus and gave him all that they had. We weren't even old friends; they had known us for only those fourteen days of mission.

This couple had discovered that however limited our personal wealth may be it still needs to be under the control of the King. As Jesus said, 'It is much harder for a rich person to enter the Kingdom of God than for a camel to go through the eye of a needle' (Mark 10:25). Those to whom God has given any degree of personal wealth will have to surrender the control of those resources to the Lord if they are to avoid the corrupting influence of our times and truly live the life of the Kingdom.

Jesus said, 'No one can be a slave of two masters . . . you cannot serve both God and money, (Matt. 6:24), and this refers to all the facets of material wealth. God may give us these things but we need to hold them lightly because of the corrupting influence which they can exert on our hearts. If we recognise that they are God's gifts to us and that he can require them back from us as easily as he gave them, then we will not fall into the trap of assigning to them a wrong position in our hearts.

You see Satan's attack is so insidious at this point, that we don't even realise what is happening. Then one morning we wake up and God prompts us to ask, 'What have we given to others in need? What needs have we noticed in the last month? What has God directed us towards in terms of our giving?'

Then we realise how cold we have become. If others accused us we would never accept that there was a weakness here. Yet our cold hearts condemn us. Possessions are not of God when they blind our hearts to his prompting, our eyes to the needs of others and our will to meet those needs with what the Lord has given us, on loan, from him.

Discrimination

It is interesting to note our conversation with strangers. Normally we begin by asking for a name, then we enquire about occupation. Identity is swiftly established by how we earn our living. The life-style of the Kingdom speaks for a different standard of values.

Jesus has made each of us unique individuals with different gifts and abilities. We are all important, whatever our occupation, wealth or status may be. We are taught not to make instant value judgments but to esteem each other higher than ourselves. The world looks to prestige or wealth as establishing value but we are not to act like that.

The less wealthy are not to give artificial status to somebody just because they are wealthy. If Jesus spent his life with the poor, as he did, then we are not to wrongly cultivate a man just because he is materially rich. 'My brothers . . . you must never treat people in different ways according to their outward appearance. Suppose a rich man wearing a gold ring and fine clothes comes to your meeting, and a poor man in ragged clothes also comes. If you show more respect to the well-dressed man and say to him, "Have this best seat here," but you say to the poor man, "Stand over there, or sit here on the floor by my feet," then you are guilty of creating distinctions among yourselves' (Jas. 2:1–4). As William Barclay has said:

'It is not that Christ and the Church do not want the great and the rich and the wise and the mighty: we must be aware of an inverted snobbery . . . but it was the simple fact that the Gospel offered so much to the poor, and demands so much from the rich, that it was the poor who were swept into the Church. It was, in fact, the common people who heard Jesus gladly, and the rich young ruler who went away sorrowfully because he had great possessions.'[3]

So we must be careful not to discriminate either in favour or against the rich. The radical nature of the Christian gospel is seen in the fact that all are brothers and sisters, regardless of background or personal wealth. We must be careful not to be guilty of making class distinctions when all are people made by God and equal before him in creation.

Nor must we condemn a man because he is rich. Often we are motivated by petty jealousy. True, a man can gain wealth by exploitation, but it can also come as a result of God's favour towards a man over whom he has control. Many of us lack wealth because God couldn't trust us with it! I have had the privilege of meeting many relatively wealthy christian businessmen. One I will never forget was twisted inside by his success and had little concern for others. Many, however, have shown me the ways and love of Jesus, deeply challenging my own life through their deep, personal surrender of their wealth to the Lord of Glory. All success and provision is seen as the gift of God rather than any merit of their own! And those that could not share that attitude were learning to do so!!

Whatever our personal wealth we must be careful of any feeling of superiority towards others, because that is the prevailing pressure of our age. So often Christianity is middle-class and alienated from the people with whom Jesus spent his life. Too often when the immigrants move into the inner city the Christians move out! We desert the cities for the comforts of suburbia and only commute into our old church base for worship.

The time has come within our nation to move back in and reclaim the ground which we have left. Often Christian commitment has meant for a working-class man a multitude of hidden pressures towards so-called social betterment. The Christian ethic has led us to hard work and therefore increased money but it must never result in us losing our roots.

We have been guilty of most awful discrimination:

i) In leaving the cities, we have abandoned them to the forces of Satan or a mere 'social gospel'.

ii) In seeking to constantly better ourselves, we have forgotten that Jesus introduced his mission by being incarnate in the world of the poor. Born in a stable, into a poor peasant carpenter's family, leaving unfashionable Nazareth which was despised by the social hierarchy of the day to speak of the King and the Kingdom.

iii) We have not identified ourselves with the struggles of the poor and oppressed. Our gospel has been one of another heavenly world, we have said little to challenge the social structures of our generation.

iv) We have failed to stand alongside those of other race or culture. Our churches have been 'white' or 'black' and we have therefore failed to make a powerful statement to our society of a Kingdom which has no concept of discrimination into rich or poor, black or white.

'Evangelicals need to remember that we have to earn the right of hearing of the gospel in our modern world. When we remain in our places of privilege we are placing a barrier between ourselves and our brothers and sisters in the Third World, or in the great inner-city populations of our urban industrial societies in the West for whom Christ died. Incarnational Christianity means putting ourselves at risk. It means sacrificing our privileged life-styles and identifying with the deprived and powerless, in order to become channels of the creative power of Christ.'[4]

As Abraham Lincoln observed, 'God must love the common people because he made so many of them.' For some of us the answer to discrimination will lie in a new commitment to return to the cities; for others to gain a new recognition of one another whatever our so-called social status may be. For all of us it must mean the creation of the Kingdom in our attitudes to each other wherein we can see rich and poor sharing together the life of Jesus.

Sharing

The gospel of Jesus was especially valuable to the weak and oppressed, the poor and needy. Within it was a welcome for those with none to welcome them and a value on those the world holds as valueless. In the society of James' day the rich oppressed the poor, dragging them to the law courts, debts were recalled at extortionate rates and the poor could scarcely live. There was a common practise of a creditor seizing a debtor by the neck of his robe, nearly throttling him and dragging him to court. James never condemned riches, but the conduct of riches without sympathy!

It was the same in the Old Testament. 'If there is among you a poor man, one of your brethren, in any of your towns . . . you shall not harden your heart or shut your hand against your poor brother' (Deut. 15:7 RSV). If we want our society to believe that we have met the living God, then mere words will not be enough. They will need to see an alternative style of living which demonstrates the fact! As John succinctly put it, 'This is how we know what love is: Christ gave his life for us. We too, then, ought to give our lives for our brothers! If a rich person sees his brother in need, yet closes his heart against his brother, how can he claim that he loves God? My children, our love should not be just words and talk; it must be true love, which shows itself in action' (1 John 3:16–18 GNB).

We are called to communal living whether we like it or not!

I am not suggesting that we should all merge into an extended family or even a closed community. That is a specific call from God. However, we do need to be far more aware of the needs of each other.

'It would be a mistake to limit the concept of "community" either to the traditional and special monastic orders or to the more recent development of extended households. God calls all his people to become the community of God, even though obviously the levels of commitment within that community will necessarily vary continually.'[5]

There is so much that we can share. Our car, washing machine, freezer, tools, garden-hose, the list is endless. The more we can share together, the greater our contact, and the more funds which can be released for the work of the Kingdom! We can also share our money and that is another thing that the world will never be able to understand.

A Christian friend found himself in deep financial difficulty. Instead of turning for help, exposing his need and making himself vulnerable, he tried embezzling the money he needed. He firmly intended to repay the money and made little attempt to hide the discrepancy. Discovered by his employers he was jailed for embezzlement. Many Christians tried to help. Some visited his wife and family, some prayed and shared with him, some sympathised, but one acted in a unique way. He and his wife made the man a long-term loan so he could repay the stolen cash and potentially reduce his sentence, and also provided a job. Such is the nature of genuine Christian trust and sharing together.

Whenever a Christian, or group of Christians, is in need, not of their own making, we should have a real sense of corporate responsibility. For example, Paul thanks the Philipians for all their gifts and help which was such a relief to the Church in Jerusalem when they faced the crisis of famine. Such is a real demonstration of loving friendship in the body of Christ.

This is never a one-way traffic. We should never keep, as it were, a profit and loss account. If we freely give to others then the Lord has a habit of freely providing for us. 'Give to others, and God will give to you. Indeed, you will receive a full measure, a generous helping, poured into your hands – all that you can hold. The measure you use for others is the one that God will use for you' (Luke 6:38).

Giving

I recognise that any child of the King of Kings must expect him to want everything. God is only a capitalist in this one instance; he demands a take-over bid of the totality of our lives! So technically, once we have surrendered to Jesus, then everything we have and are belong to him.

Now this is great in theory. Throughout the Scriptures God demanded some very active practice to demonstrate that the principle was being lived out.

i) His people were to give 10 per cent from their labours and were to give it to the Lord. 'Set aside a tithe – a tenth of all that your fields produce each year' (Deut. 14:22). This was certainly no suggestion but a direct command.

ii) He didn't mind receiving it in cash. 'If the place of worship is too far from your home for you to carry there the tithe of the produce that the Lord blessed you with . . . then . . . Sell your produce and take the money' (Deut. 14:24). I once heard an excellent definition of tithing by which any of us will know whether or not we are being obedient in this matter. The question was asked, 'If God gave you ten times what you give him, could you live on it?'

iii) Tithing is not really the same as giving, it is God's tax. Once we have written off our tenth, a good practise for the start of a new year, then we can start to give to the Lord. Wave offerings, thank offerings, drink offerings, cereal offerings, all came on top of the tithe. One good way, which many practise, is to make out bank standing orders and covenant forms in January, giving away the one-tenth required to be paid by standing order over the year so that our offerings can then come via our cash or cheque book on top of the tithe, as the Lord provides during the year.

iv) It is not the amount we give but the cost and sacrifice which lies behind it which concerns the Lord. He is much more concerned with the percentage it represents of what we could give, than the actual amount involved. 'They gave as much as they could' (Ezra 2:69). 'He looked up and saw the rich putting their gifts into the treasury; and he saw a poor widow put in two copper coins. And he said, "Truly I tell you, this poor widow has put in more than all of them; for they all contributed out of their abundance, but she out of her poverty put in all the living that she had" (Luke 21:1–4 RSV).

v) God is concerned about the attitude which lies behind the way we give. We must never give in order to try and earn God's favour, but rather to seek to express our love and gratitude to him. 'They offered great sacrifices that day and rejoiced.' God doesn't want his people to give on an emotional high and then regret it, but he does want his people to give in order that he might give to them. 'One man gives freely, yet grows all the richer; another witholds what he should give, and only suffers want.' (Prov. 11:24 RSV). 'Speak to the people of Israel, that they take for me an offering; from every man whose heart makes him willing you shall receive the offering for me' (Exod. 25:2 RSV). 'The people rejoiced because these had given willingly' (1 Chr. 29:9 RSV), which goes on to say, 'for with a whole heart they had offered freely to the Lord.'

vi) There are no special case exceptions to the rule! Even if we are clergy who receive tithed money the Lord has a word for us. 'When you receive from the Israelites the tithe that the Lord gives you as your possession, you must present a tenth of it as a special contribution to the Lord' (Num. 18:26 GNB).

There are over seven hundred references to giving in the Old and New Testaments. The New Testament has more to say about giving than the return of Jesus Christ! It's an important emphasis which can be summarised in two statements. 'Honour the Lord by making him an offering from the best' (Prov. 3:9). 'God loves the one who gives gladly' (2 Cor. 9:7).

But giving is a two-way process and God loves to give to us, far, far more than we can ever imagine! God created this world, the material was his creation and in Genesis he said it was good (Gen. 1:31). For that reason God can reward those who he loves with material prosperity! 'The Lord made him prosperous again and gave him twice as much as he had had before' (Job 42:10).

A few years ago I left my wife at home and went away for ten days mission in Newcastle. We were not on the telephone. Unknown to me my wife's bank account was empty, and she had only ten pence in her purse and an empty larder. Day after day she asked

the Lord to send her money, as he did so regularly
for us. But he never responded in that way. Instead,
day after day, without her speaking to anybody about
it, someone would come to drive her to college, in-
vitations came for a meal, and food arrived on the
doorstep! Ten days later the Lord sent thirty pounds
just to show Ruth he could do that. For seven years
we never again had goods arrive like that. When I
returned from Newcastle Ruth gave me the ten pence
– she had never lacked for anything.

Generosity

The Christian reason for giving generously to God lies
in the fact that God has been so tremendously generous to us. The thrill of recognising all that Jesus has
done for us naturally results in our wanting to give
everything to him.

The results are often delightfully extravagant. Zacchaeus gave away half of all he possessed; the woman
who anointed Jesus' feet poured out the whole bottle;
the Macedonian Christian Fellowship gave more than
they could afford to aid the Church in Jerusalem. As
Eric Delve succinctly puts it, 'There are few things
so exciting or liberating as giving money away. It is
a delightfully anarchistic thing to do in our greedy
society.'[6]

J. B. Phillips has paraphrased 2 Corinthians 9:15
in this way. 'Thank God, then, for his indescribable
generosity to you!' God himself has given the example; it's time we followed.

We need, however, to be careful where we give.
There are many demands. Take these six for example.
Each are worthy, in varying degrees, and we need to
ask God how he would have us divide our giving.
a) The cause of mission and evangelism overseas.
b) The maintenance of church buildings.

c) The vicar's or pastor's salary (which Paul suggests in 1 Timothy 5:17–18 should be twice the normal!)

d) The needs of mission and evangelism in our own country.

e) To help the hungry and deprived.

f) To finance the central bureaucracy of a church or denomination (ask first what they want to spend it on!).

Too many of us glibly pass our giving for others to administer. We should ensure that we are hearing how God wants us to apportion our giving and where God wants it to go. If you choose to administer your own giving then that's easy; but many give their total contribution to their church so that the rightful tax refund on covenant may be obtained. If this is your position, then many church treasurers will receive your direction on where you want your giving to go each year. If not, then special Christian Trusts like UK Evangelisation Trust, Macedonian Trust, or a secular body like Charities Aid will gladly do so. The same covenant facilities will, of course, be available.

The reason for this practical guidance is to encourage us not to abdicate our responsibilities to give as God directs us. As the apostle Paul summarises it, 'Remember that the person who sows few seeds will have a small crop; the one who sows many seeds will have a large crop. Each one should give, then, as he has decided, not with regret or out of a sense of duty . . . and God is able to give you more than you need, so that you will always have all you need for yourselves and more than enough for every good cause' (2 Cor. 9:6–8).

The story is told how, many years ago, there was a man who had absolutely nothing. But God who loved him gave him ten apples. He gave him the first three apples so that the man would have something nice to eat. God gave the man the second three apples so that he would have something to trade in order to get a place to live. He gave him the third three apples so that he could trade them for something to wear. God gave him the last apple so that he would have something to give back in gratitude for the other nine.

The man devoured the first three apples and they were delightful. He traded the second three and got himself somewhere to live. He traded the other three apples and got himself something nice to wear. Then he came to the tenth apple. Now he knew that God had given him the tenth apple so that he would have something to give back to God in appreciation for the other nine.

The trouble was, the longer he looked at the tenth apple, the bigger and juicier it appeared. He began to think that, after all, God owned all the apples in the world so one more or less wouldn't matter.

So the man did what so many of us have done. He ate the tenth apple and gave God the core![7]

6: A Passion for Souls

There is one thing which Christians and non-Christians have in common: we're both up-tight about evangelism. It was Rebecca Manley Pippert who first introduced the thought which many have recognised to be true; there is something about the idea of sharing our faith with other people which seems to create mental and emotional blockages like nothing else on earth![1]

Embarrassed . . . alienated . . . condemned . . . confused. Don't worry – you're not the only one who feels that way about evangelism. Worship, prayer, church involvement, Bible-reading – nothing else seems to create the tangled web of emotional reactions which the word 'evangelism' conjures up for so many of us.

The problems generated by our own sense of inadequacy and insecurity are covered by a thin veneer of excuses. 'It's not my gift.' 'We're having a mission next year.' Somehow a deep commitment to share the message of Jesus with others seems to smack of fanaticism. Yet a fanatic has been defined as only a person who loves Jesus more than I do!

Deep down we feel guilty . . .

Guilty because we suspect that we are failing in our duty to God himself.

Guilty because we feel condemned by the stories of

all the great saints of God (past and present and generally as humanly inadequate as you and I) who served the Lord in outstanding ways.

Guilty because we recognise all the opportunities we have managed to miss when we could have spoken naturally to others of our love for Jesus.

Guilty because we know that people should be aware of a direct road to a deep and personal commitment to God himself, but most have never heard that message for themselves.

Guilty because we failed to protest when society reinstated sex and politics to general conversation but continued to dismiss religion as an unacceptable item on the agenda.

Guilty because we are often more embarrassed when Jesus is talked about than is the non-Christian.

Yes, deep down we feel guilty.

However, our cover-up job has been very effective. We faced two alternatives. Either we freely confessed our weakness and gained divine forgiveness and strength to meet the spiritual needs of our land. Or we could build our own structures which would look as if we were achieving our aims but, in fact, ensured that we were well back from the front line.

Tragically we settled for the latter. We covered the message of Jesus for ordinary people today with a vocabulary which rendered it utterly meaningless to the vast majority of the population.

We paid others to conduct missions and campaigns, to share the Christian message and fulfil the task which Jesus had entrusted to *us*.

We enclosed this proclamation in our own buildings, tents and meetings, largely excluding the non-Christian from ever hearing the good news.

We created a Christian culture to ensure that anyone who embraced our gospel would also fit into our society. No longer could anyone just commit their lives to Jesus Christ; the norms and standards of evangelical church-goers had to be received as well.

We divided our lives into their secular and spiritual dimensions. Our spiritual lives concerned our relationship with the Lord while our times of work and leisure were labelled 'secular'. The danger was that we only expected the Lord to use the 'spiritual' dimension, when in fact our 'secular' activities gave far more scope for Christian witness.

Feelings of guilt invariably provoke a response. It is so sad that our own sense of guilt should contribute to our alienation from the bulk of society today. The heart of God aches for a world which still rejects him while our lives seem to be devoted to preserving the status quo.

The story is told of a preacher who was walking along a street in Soho and passed by a strip club. He sensed a clear word from God to himself: 'Stop. Go into the strip club.' Immediately he dismissed the thought as the product of a sinful imagination.

'Stop. Go into the strip club. Go up to the go-go dancer and tell her that I love her.'

He was a mature Christian who knew the voice of God and that resistance was useless. So, taking a quick look round to make sure no one was watching, he paid his entrance fee and went in! He didn't know where to look. So he walked straight up to the front and told the go-go dancer that Jesus loved her.

'Hey! You sit down there, I wanna talk to you.' Her reply amazed him. So he waited while she dressed and came to talk. In simple terms he told her about Jesus. In halting phrases she explained how, over the last few days, a hunger had grown to discover the love and affection of the living God.

Now that preacher's obedience made him break all

the rules. He spoke simply in her language. He obeyed God himself, not trying to hide behind the gift and experience of others who might be used to help girls in that tragic profession. He met her on her own ground, which was as far from the Church as you could go. He didn't condemn her, or impose extra-biblical demands on her commitment to Jesus. He didn't protest that God couldn't use him because the situation and timing were wrong. He was simply obedient, and he led the girl to Jesus!

Too many will find the story objectionable, but how different is it to the story of the one who set the example for us all? 'A Pharisee invited Jesus to have dinner with him . . . In that town was a woman who lived a sinful life . . . she brought an alabaster jar full of perfume and stood behind Jesus, by his feet, crying and wetting his feet with her tears. Then she dried his feet with her hair, kissed them, and poured the perfume on them! (Luke 7:36–38). When the Pharisee wondered to himself how Jesus could let an immoral woman make such a disgusting exhibition of affection for him, Jesus told him how he had failed in his duties as a host. He had failed to care for Jesus' bodily needs so a sinner had done so. Why? Because she had been forgiven much and knew her need. Simon, the Pharisee, had little awareness of his sin and so showed little love. How dare we emulate the Pharisees by showing all-consuming commitment to our little traditions and meetings while our workmates, neighbours, and our world, go to Hell!

'No one lights a lamp and then hides it or puts it under a bowl; instead he puts it on the lampstand. . . . Make certain, then, that the light in you is not darkness' (Luke 11:33–35). Jesus has placed us here as lights in a dark world, to demonstrate through our lives, our words, our acts of kindness and mercy that he is alive and at work in us. He never intended that we should hide from the world but rather that we should be at work in the middle of it. We have no right to create a cosy evangelical ghetto to protect us from society. If we do not share and tell of Jesus, who will?

As Jesus said, 'How terrible for you. . . . You have kept the key that opens the door to the house of knowledge; you yourselves will not go in, and you stop those who are trying to go in!' (Luke 11:52).

'I'm sorry, sir. I suppose you are aware that you were travelling in the wrong direction down a one-way street?' I don't know if it's ever happened to you. It certainly has to me. That moment of confusion when you have to explain in all honesty to a blue-uniformed gentleman that you just didn't see the sign.

Of course road-signs are necessary. Yet I breathe a sigh of relief when I reach a clearway or motorway and face the minimum of warning signs to contend with. The Christian life is a journey, a road which we are called to travel. The Lord has placed the minimum number of road-signs in our path. Yet, when we invite others to begin to travel along the road, we manage to devise signs which seem deliberately to create obstacles to their progress.

So many are searching for a pathway through life which they have never discovered. As a working evangelist I have noticed, particularly in the last three years, that the tide seems to be turning in Britain. There seems a genuine resurgence of interest in the message of Jesus and a growing rejection of alternatives. Many are taking a quiet look at their lives and objectives, and are coming up with disturbing answers.

Only the dark and a lone hound's baying,
The hunger's horn in the ancient call,

129

Sounds in the brush and hidden eyes watching,
A presence felt, a following footfall.

Wind in my face and a cold rain's falling,
Moan of the surf on the desolate shore,
Loneliness, Christ, and the long trail's ending,
Mountains behind me, mists before.

Never a word or a kiss of friendship,
Never a sunrise, never a lark,
Never a dawn for my eyes to witness,
Only the dark.

The poem's title is – *Motive for suicide*; the writer – an eighteen-year-old girl in a mental hospital. I would not want to be so facile as to suggest that all non-Christians live in abject misery. Or that everybody has reached the same state of desperation as this girl. Yet many have come to a growing sense that somehow life is a little sour and that there must be something more than mere existence.

Most people enjoy their sin – at least I know I did! It's great to do your own thing. But then you come to a time when you start to realise the effects of your selfishness on others, to recognise the damage that your life can do to people around you. It is at such times that a caring, sympathetic Christian's ear, which has heard our shouts of sinful enjoyment, can also hear our cry of quiet panic and present the message of the living God. The message of a God who cares for and loves each individual and who can introduce them to himself.

It was the work of total self-giving love to break down the divide which man's sinful self-will brought between him and God. When God poured out his own blood in the person of his Son, on a cross, he earned once and for all the right to forgive, cleanse, indwell and direct the lives of every individual who would surrender themselves to him.

Beneath the garish trappings of our present-day materialistic society, there still lurks the plaintive cry of men and women looking for God. There comes a time in everybody's life when the love of God would draw them to himself. We need to hear the cry and listen. By our caring concern, which is not exhibited so much in our talking as our listening, we will reflect the love of Jesus.

By so doing we will help to erect three very positive road signs to enable our non-Christian friends and neighbours to discover what the Christian life is all about.

One-way traffic

The first sign is an obvious one. But it is one about which, with the alternative gods who offer themselves today for our worship, we need to be reminded. There is only one way to God, and that lies through the simple offering of our lives to the love and direction of his Son.

Keep left (right if symbol reversed)

It is important to recognise that for as long as we keep our eyes on Jesus he will keep us to the correct side of the road. The Christian life does not leave room for compromise. As the prophet Elijah demanded, 'How much longer will it take you to make up your minds?' (1 Kgs. 18:21). If we claim to be travelling towards Jesus but find ourselves on the wrong side of the road, then we're likely to get mown down by oncoming traffic!

Minimum speed

The Christian life is not a matter of slowly struggling on by our own efforts. Nor is it a stop-start, stop-start process. If we want to be of real service to the Lord, then we need to get a move on in our relationship with him. There need be no speed limit for our surrendering to the will of

God. By giving him all that we have and are, right at the beginning, we can experience the full, joyful surge of Spirit-filled living.

Instead of using these very positive signs, we seem to have concentrated on the negative! We have demanded of all newly-committed Christians that they obey our series of prohibitions, rather than get involved with people where they are. There is one thing that we lose when we commit ourselves to Jesus Christ. Each year reduces the number of our non-Christian friends and contacts. Therefore, rather than burden young Christians with all that they should not be doing, we must actively encourage them to get on with the job in hand.

Jesus told the disciples that 'You are witnesses' (Luke 24:48). He clearly instructed them, 'Go, then, to all peoples everywhere and make them my disciples' (Matt. 28:18).

Instead, we erect our regulations for young Christians:

 a) Slow down – you'll overtake us if you don't.

b) Make sure you give way to our patterns and traditions.

 c) A church can often be like a private club – be careful who you introduce.

d) This is the speed at which this church is going. It is the maximum – don't go any faster or you'll embarrass the rest of us!

e) Stop it – we just don't do that kind of thing here!

 f) If you threaten to go further in your Christian life and see greater blessing than our leaders, you'll threaten the structure.

g) Wrong direction!

h) Basically, it's just not the kind of place we feel you should go to any more.

i) We're all pedestrians here! Supercharged or motorised vehicles are not our style.

No motor vehicles

j) We've always gone in this direction and we don't feel it's right to disturb the status quo or rock the boat with any deviation.

No right turn

It would be so easy to descend into a combination of cynicism and despair . . . to write off the Church . . . to try to start again. Perhaps it would be more honest to ask how we have arrived at the present state of affairs?

i) Why have so few, in this so-called 'Christian' country, any real understanding of the Christian message?

ii) Why do so many Christians seek to avoid those very areas of our society where people are visibly showing their hurt and pain?

iii) Why are we so concerned to stereotype ourselves? Why do we try to reduce all the diverse gifts and enthusiasms of young Christians to the predictable level of a generation of 'evangelical Homepride flour graders coming off a conveyor belt?'

iv) Why do we concentrate so many of our activities around a church building, when we live in a society which has clearly rejected the Church as it sees it; but who might be very open to the message of a Jesus who loves and dies for them?

Could it be that a series of wrong attitudes on our part have created road blocks between us, as the Church of Christ, and the world for which he died?

Roadblock 1: *Survivalism*

A. W. Tozer rightly comments, 'The Church began in power, moved in power, and moved just as long as she had power. When she no longer had power she dug in for safety and sought to conserve her gains.'[2] Christian history has always been divided into two phases, the dynamic and the static. In the former, men and women took risks in God, fearlessly communicating his love and truth to a largely hostile world. Exchanging the safety of inaction for the hazards of God inspired progress as they discovered that the power and miracles of God went with them.

In more static periods, like that in which we live today, things are somewhat different. The odds appear overwhelming and, tired of the struggle, the people of God have settled for a life of peace and security. The emphasis has changed to preserving our structure of meetings, our patterns of worship, our church membership – all the more peripheral issues assume prime importance!

Much of the reason for these attitudes lies in a deep-rooted fear that our decline, if continued without check, would rest in the extinction of the Christian faith in our country. Safety is found in the traditional, even when it has already clearly failed to reverse the trend of decline! Change, experiment, pioneering methods or ideas are frowned upon. The emphasis is entirely on survival, anything that threatens our continuation in well-worn paths is firmly resisted.

The tragedy is that while the Baptist Union admits that it takes four Baptists five years to bring one person to Christ, we recline in glib self-satisfaction. We can so easily forget that God will not preserve his Church by blessing the efforts which we make on his behalf. He wants us to sense his divinely-ordained purposes and join in! Because our Lord is a creative

God he is constantly developing new things! 'Now I tell you of new things to come, events that I did not reveal before. Only now am I making them happen; nothing like this took place in the past.' God then explains the reason why he is only now telling his people. 'If it had, you would claim that you knew all about it. I knew that you couldn't be trusted' (Isa. 48:6–8).

The problem has always been the same: we are afraid to venture out in God and take risks, we love to keep to established paths because then we can claim the credit for ourselves! God, on the other hand, longs to demonstrate his own authority and glory by doing the unexpected among his people.

Roadblock 2: *Arrogance*

'My God's not dead, sorry about yours!' This kind of supercilious evangelical arrogance shouted a message to me from the car rear window. I'm afraid that it was scarcely the message intended.

An overwhelming concern for the spiritual needs of our friends and neighbours can rarely be conveyed in comments as unwise as this.

Jesus never adopted these kinds of superior attitudes. He never comfortably relaxed into the attitude that he was OK so the rest of the world could go to Hell. Jesus burned out his life serving, not the righteous but the sinners. He also spoke of his Father's caring commitment to prodigals! 'He was still a long way from home when his father saw him; his heart was filled with pity, and he ran, threw his arms round his son, and kissed him' (Luke 15:20).

God doesn't have first- and second-class sons. He has a role and gifts for each one of us. He longs that we might fit into a glorious many-membered body which will demonstrate his love and compassion to the world at large.

Far from separating himself, hiding away in a corner, God is full of love and compassion, longing to welcome men and women back to himself. The Greek word which Jesus used for compassion is *splangchnizegthai*. The word is important because it does not refer to a superficial concern. The word means a heart-breaking love which comes from the kidneys, liver and intestines – a gut-level love.

God's love is so clear. When the prodigal returned the father heard his cry, felt a depth of love and, demonstrating his care for the runaway son, he served the prodigal, giving him gifts and a massive welcome home celebration.

The attitude of his older son was very different. This one sulked in the shadows resenting the forgiveness of the father. How like those of us who are Christians today! We can't understand how the Lord can still love, with a breaking heart, this fallen world. We show our disapproval by cutting ourselves off, as far as possible, from any possibility of demonstrating servant-hood to those who reject the living God. The fact is that we are all sinners, but there are two great classes of sins. We are all familiar with sins of the body such as those committed by the prodigal. But many of us are far less ready to recognise and condemn the sin of the elder brother because we suspect that we could be equally guilty!

'Look at the elder brother – moral, hard-working, patient, dutiful – let him get all credit for his virtue. Look at this man, this baby, sulking on his father's own door. "He was angry," we read, "and would not go in." Look at the effect upon the father, upon the servants, upon the happiness of the guests. Judge of the effect upon the prodigal –

and how many prodigals are kept out of the Kingdom of God by the unlovely character of those who
profess to be inside.'[3]

Roadblock 3: *Isolation*

Those same fears and insecurities which have persuaded us to be content with the familiar have also
been quick to warn us of the danger of meeting the
world on its own ground!

Consequently, we have been content to shout our
slogans at a distance, or to invite people to come and
hear our message – but in our style and on our territory. Little wonder then, that fewer and fewer have
rejected the Christian message – the vast majority
have never been permitted to hear it!

Our burden to reach non-Christians with the message of Jesus is too often confined to the abilities of
professionals who we pay to do the job for us. The
Early Church grew out of the spontaneous prayer,
life-style and conversation of its converts. The gospel
was chattered in the market-place and therefore
reached the people.

For this to happen again would require some fairly
radical changes. Many churches would need to reduce
the number of meetings they hold. It is possible for
some Christians to spend every night of the week at
a Christian meeting. This leaves virtually no opportunities for meeting any non-Christian outside of
working hours. It has also tended to make Christians
identify their lives in two segments: the secular, i.e.
work; the spiritual, leisure time, that is, church activities. This division leaves us with no time to share our
lives, let alone our words, with non-Christians.

It also means that a number of us will have to adjust
our attitude towards certain places which have been
forbidden to Christians until recent years. A friend of

mine who is a Baptist minister visits his local pub every week. He has to – he captains the darts team! At least part of the rapid growth in his congregation must be due to the wide range of contacts created by his extra-curricula activities!

Once upon a time the centre of the community (as far as the young wives were concerned) was the village well. Today it's the school gate. One has only to see and hear the conversation of young mums at the start or finish of the school day to realise the opportunities which exist there to chatter the gospel of Jesus. Both the launderette and the supermarket create similar opportunities. For men, there's always the working men's club or the pub.

There is community involvement in local politics, or the parent/teacher association; participation in local radio or the community newspaper. School, college and work offer countless opportunities. One friend became a committed Christian through the witness of a fifteen-year-old girl and the patient sharing of a number of older Christians. He went back to school full of fire and enthusiasm. The Christian Union was revolutionised by this one young convert. In the weeks which followed dozens at the school committed their lives to Jesus Christ. One, at least, is a full-time evangelist today because of the work and witness of a schoolboy who met Jesus and couldn't bear to keep his faith hidden in a corner.

Of course we need to exercise a degree of caution. We need to be brutally honest with ourselves. To go to the pub claiming our motive as witness when really we are thirsty would be blasphemy of the worst kind. We need to surround ourselves with prayer, never to venture into Satan's strongholds alone but always with at least one companion to support us, and we need to be careful only to go to those places where God has given us his own encouragement and authority to identify with others and to serve him.

I will never forget being in a bar with my co-author, Eric Delve. A rather loud businessman proclaimed to his two friends that Christianity had nothing to say. Eric took the next hour to prove that it had an awful lot to say. The businessman enjoyed a good argument – his friends heard the gospel as they'd never heard it before!

Roadblock 4: *Social Divorce*

For centuries the state has used Christianity for its own purposes. It has been abused and misused to provide an ideological glue to hold the state together. Therefore it only took a few phrases from Archbishop Runcie to throw our national newspapers into turmoil at the mere suggestion that our every motive and action in the Falklands conflict, for example, was not morally justified by our national activity.

Jesus was accused with charges of a political nature. 'We caught this man misleading our people, telling them not to pay taxes to the Emperor and claiming that he himself is the Messiah, a king' (Luke 23:2). These charges of blasphemy and sedition were similarly levelled against the early missionaries. 'They are all breaking the laws of the Emperor, saying that there is another king, whose name is Jesus' (Acts 17:7).

To truly proclaim the message of Jesus is to draw the conclusion that he died for the whole of society rather than any one particular section. To allow ourselves to be bound by conventions on what we should, or should not talk about, to blindly follow the political doctrines of our peers – these are attitudes which will only serve to divorce us from a large section of our world.

The people of God, in both the Old and New

Testaments, clearly lived out an economic alternative to the rest of the world which surrounded them. Instead of looking only to their own affairs they clearly cared for others, and by so doing they proclaimed the reign and rule of Jesus in their lives. So much so that it was clearly noted: 'There was no one in the group who was in need' (Acts 4:34).

The prophets clearly warned that piety, proper religion and ritual observance could never be adequate in the eyes of God. If we are to have anything to say to our friends and neighbours we must first earn the right to say it. Amos demanded that we stand as advocates of justice (Amos 5:21–24). Isaiah tells us that the fast in which God delights involves breaking the yoke of oppression, sharing our bread with the hungry, and bringing the homeless poor into our homes (Isa. 58:5–7). Jesus testified in answer to queries of his messiahship that 'the blind can see, the lame can walk, the (lepers) are made clean, the deaf hear, the dead are brought back to life, and the Good News is preached to the poor' (Matt. 11:4).

The parable of the Good Samaritan clearly shows that human danger, or worries, overtime, money, race or class, need to be subordinated to our responsibility for others. The apostles repeatedly claim that faith without works that demonstrate obedience is dead, that the quality of our love for God is shown in the personal and practical love which we show towards others around us.

In part, that love is truly demonstrated only when we are prepared to meet others on their ground rather than demand that they visit ours.

On one occasion my wife and I were invited to spend the evening with neighbours. Now, culturally, that invitation to us meant dinner. So we starved all day anticipating a highly calorific evening. When we arrived at our neighbour's home we were warmly welcomed and offered both something to drink and a bowl of assorted crisps and nuts. But we couldn't smell anything cooking or see evidence of a salad. The process was repeated several times over the evening but no more substantial food arrived.

The reason was simple. My wife and I would recreate a restaurant in our home. Our friends re-created the pub! Being in surroundings where they felt relaxed they freely shared their needs and lack of faith. It gave a tremendous opportunity to talk about Jesus and all because we were on their ground, rather than they on ours!

Too often our priorities have rested in our own selfish motives or desire to avoid embarrassment. In total contrast was the life of the only one who ever had the right to choose his life-style and birth-place. Jesus chose a cattle-trough in a stable, the life of an artisan, the humiliation of rejection by his countrymen and death upon a Roman gibbet sited on a Jerusalem rubbish dump. He rarely conformed to the patterns which religious men demanded of him. 'Why do you eat and drink with tax collectors and other outcasts?' (Luke 5:30). 'He is a glutton and a drinker, a friend of tax collectors and other outcasts' (Luke 7:34). 'This man has gone as a guest to the home of a sinner' (Luke 19:7). What a testimony to the love and kindness of God's Son. Time and again he was criticised for mixing with the wrong people.

We have no scriptural precedent for inviting people into our buildings or tents or on to our territory to hear the Christian message. Nor do we have any justification for putting the preacher six feet up in the air, way above contradiction! These things can, at best, only be a back-up to our personal sharing of Jesus with people where they are. At worst they can be further evidence of our monumental arrogance in demanding that people come to us to hear our message.

Jesus met with people simply where they were and incurred the displeasure of the religious leaders for exposing their failure to do so. The same will happen today, but then Jesus concluded, 'Woe to you, when all men speak well of you' (Luke 6:26 RSV). The important thing for Jesus was that sinners heard him gladly!

Do we mix with the wrong people? Do we seize our opportunities to live and to chatter the gospel? Do we allow the Lord to use us or do we abdicate our responsibilities and try to pass them on to others?

For some of us it will be our kindness, for others the joyful freedom on our faces and in our lives. For some of us the love and concern of our prayer lives will break out in our compassion, others of us will gossip the gospel. But each one of us has a responsibility and a function.

The story is told of two men who had worked together in a factory for ten years. One arrived for work looking somewhat sheepish that morning. With a real effort he plucked up his courage and stammered out, 'I think I ought to tell you that I've become a Christian.'

'Praise the Lord,' replied his colleague.

'What on earth do you mean?'

'Why, I've been a Christian for years.'

The newly-converted factory worker was flabbergasted. His was no sudden decision. He had been struggling towards faith for years but had always looked at his friend and thought, 'Well Fred looks all right. He seems to manage without Christianity!' All those years and Fred had only to open his mouth, but never did!

7: Power from Above

Dozens of books . . . hundreds of chapters . . . thousands of sentences and tens of thousands of words. So much has been poured out about the person and work of the Holy Spirit. Pentecostal, non-Pentecostal, Catholic, Evangelical, Charismatic, anti-Charismatic – all have attempted their own definitive treatments. Few conclusions have been drawn. Many heated words have been spoken.

'Fanatic, second-class Christian, over-emotional, unbiblical.' Such terms are multiplied in an internal warfare which might appear to an outside observer as confusion over terminology and experience. Too often, on close examination, the problems lie more in misunderstanding and failure to hear one another than in genuine issues. Frequently it seems that opposition to the view-point of another is aroused more by personal insecurity than from genuine hurt or grievance. Certainly the charismatic controversy must rank as a gaping wound in the body of Christ. The only victor would appear to be the Devil himself.

He has succeeded on two counts. On the one hand he has frightened many Christians away from seeking a more intimate relationship with the Holy Spirit; on the other, he has diverted the attention of spiritually motivated people away from the needs of society and towards the failings of their brothers and sisters. Too often this has led to Christians directly doing the Devil's work for him, both criticising and persecuting one another!

Greek mythology tells of an innkeeper named Procrustes. He had only one bed of fixed length on which all visitors were forced to lie. Procrustes would then cut off the feet of those who were too long and stretched the bodies of those who were too short. The result was that all visitors fitted the bed exactly, every time!

The emissaries of Church renewal often suffer the same fate as travellers in this Greek myth. On arrival they find a bed of tradition with theological legs, organisational frame and cultural mattress upon which they must lie. Unacceptable experiences are labelled enthusiastic and cut off. Unfamiliar teachings are branded heretical and stretched to fit. The price of lodging is adjustment to the status quo. Only when the bearers of renewal have enough strength to re-design the bed is there significant change.

Every year I speak at Spring Harvest, a series of training/teaching weeks in evangelism. Each week sees thousands of people of all ages gathered together in a large marquee to worship God. The beauty of it lies in the fact that everybody is free to worship God in the way that comes naturally to them. Some will have their hands in the air, others will have them firmly rooted to their pockets. Some will have smiling faces, others will wear a more serious, contemplative expression. Some will kneel, others sit; some will fix their feet to the floor while others are occasionally seen dancing up the aisles! Spontaneity and variety have replaced the demand for set responses which all must follow.

This may seem like a recipe for disorderly pandemonium. In fact, when each person's individual response is orchestrated by the Holy Spirit, it turns into a glorious reflection of that variety which exists in the body of Christ.

The tragedy is that we can feel threatened by the fact that others are so different to us. We long to make everyone conform to our pattern, otherwise our insecurities prompt us to condemn rather than commend the differences which rightly exist in the body of Christ. As Paul commented, 'If the whole body were just an eye, how could it hear?' (1 Cor. 12:17).

How dare we be responsible for seeking to stereotype the body of Christ as a structure acceptable to ourselves? How dare we seek to limit the Holy Spirit to dealing with the lives of others in the exact way that he works in our own?

I often reflect on the fact that God has made one of each of us and then thrown away the mould. This is not because he is dissatisfied with his creation, but for the very reason that he is a creator God and he hates repeating himself. The glorious diversity of both characters and gifts within the body of Christ all serve to illustrate the intense disapproval which the Lord maintains towards man-made conformity.

The Lord never wanted us just to copy each other in order to be united. Unity is not, and cannot be, the same as uniformity. After all, what could be more uniform than lines of gravestones? But a cemetery was never given to us as a model of unity!

The Lord is looking for each of us to fulfil our divine potential by making a unique contribution to the body of Christ. 'We have many parts in the one body, and all these parts have different functions. In the same way, though we are many, we are one body in union with Christ, and we are all joined to each other as different parts of one body. So we are to use our different gifts in accordance with the grace God has given us' (Rom. 12:4–6). The Holy Spirit is the divine agent of the Godhead to prepare and promote the fruit and gifts of the Spirit within us.

We can never recover our true character alone. *We* cannot repair the intrusive damage wrecked by our sinful human nature. We cannot live the life of God by our own effort. All we can do alone is try to feebly imitate some other man or woman of God. By replacing our human energies with his divine Spirit, God plans a radical purpose in each one of us. In a five-stage process he intends to restore us to all that we can be by his strength and power rather than our own.

1. Remove!

As I travel around Britain the major sin which I encounter among Christians is not jealousy, immorality or greed. It is that so many of us have a wrong view of ourselves. We examine ourselves from such a jaundiced view that we easily draw the conclusion, 'I'm useless'. We long to have the gifts of others. We struggle on with little recognition or encouragement. Increasingly we become sucked into feelings of self-pity and insecurity. We attack people God is using, we criticise and grumble. We deny the Lord the control of our lives. All because we have a wrong view of ourselves.

This has been Satan's most cunning weapon. By it he has succeeded in largely crippling the people of God, persuading us that we are more fit for a hospital than a battlefield. Where direct assault would never have succeeded, his clever strategy as the 'accuser of the brethren' has led many Christians into a morass of self-doubt and unused talents.

If the full power and potential of the living God is to be released in our lives, then there are things which must be removed by the Holy Spirit before he can do a full and complete work in us. Self-doubt, insecurity, guilt, anxiety and sin are always the prime target for his divine activity. Instead of despising ourselves, the Holy Spirit longs to reveal to us the reality that we are God's creation and that he has never devised useless creatures. Our feelings of personal inadequacy can only be removed by his gentle touch.

We are fortunate that the Lord does not deal with us all in the same way. If he did then we would spend our lives in fruitless comparisons with our fellow Christians and he would be untrue to his identity of creator. Instead, his Spirit wants to deal with each one of us in a unique work of the love of God within us. Rather than destroying our individuality, the Lord wants to restore the unique full personalities he made us to be, but blended together with one another in his body.

The Holy Spirit is no vicious tormentor intent on wrenching out of our lives those things which we have no desire to surrender. There lies the problem. He waits longingly for that moment when we will bring our guilt from the past and our anxiety for the future, placing them in his control. He patiently anticipates that time when we realise that all our sin is covered by the blood of Jesus; that we only deny Jesus the joy of Lordship of our lives by clinging on to all the bitter memories of our past defeats.

He longs to cleanse and release us from our failure. At the very moment we recognise our inability to do the will of God, we can surrender to the Holy Spirit the right to replace our feeble human struggles with a divine power and initiative which no power on earth could ever duplicate. When we then realise that by his Spirit Jesus can achieve all things within us, we discover the glorious freedom of allowing him to be

God in us. He can provide all we need, we have only to receive his provision.

2. Refill

We can only participate in all that the Lord wants to do among us when we stop demanding that God does everything in our lives at one point or another. His activity within us is ongoing and dynamic rather than once and for all and static!

When Paul wrote, 'be filled with the Spirit' (Eph. 5:18), the tense used in the original Greek is the aorist tense and does not refer to a once and for all event but an ongoing experience. A more accurate translation, (although very bad English) would be, 'Continue to be being filled with the Holy Spirit.'

Dwight L. Moody was once addressing a nineteenth century British congregation on this theme and many were offended. Afterwards several leaders and clergy took Moody to one side and demanded, 'Why do you say that we need to go on being filled with the Holy Spirit – we've been filled, twenty, or thirty years ago. Why do we need to be filled again? Moody's reply remains, to this day, an absolute classic of spiritual commonsense. 'I need to be filled with the Spirit every moment of every day – because I leak.' Today we remain a very leaky people; we desperately need to know God today, not just hark back to our memories of his activity.

A sense of holy dissatisfaction with the poverty of our knowledge of God and our love for him would quickly change the situation. No longer would we be content with merely knowing about God – we would demand a deep, intimate relationship. That very desire is prompted in our hearts by the Holy Spirit himself.

Perhaps this very response lies behind what God

has been doing in our world in recent years. As A. W. Tozer has ably summarised:

'In this hour of all-but-universal darkness one cheering gleam appears: within the fold of conservative Christianity there are to be increasing numbers of persons whose religious lives are marked by a growing hunger after God himself. They are eager for spiritual realities and will not be put off with words, nor will they be content with correct "interpretations" of truth. They are athirst for God, and they will not be satisfied till they have drunk deep at the Fountain of Living Water. This is the only real harbinger of revival which I have been able to detect anywhere on the religious horizon.'[1]

Such a generation will not waste undue prejudice or concern on the means which God employs to fill a life with his Spirit. Whether it be initially through a crisis baptism in the Holy Spirit or by progressive sanctification will not be crucial – such people will long to be filled daily.

Why? For three reasons. Firstly, in order that as individuals we might have a deep daily increase of our knowledge of God and our relationship with him. Secondly, so that those around us might clearly see that our lives are not filled with our own selfish interest but with the beauty and radiance of God himself. Thirdly, because we need that release of all the Holy Spirit would do in and through us. Until we are prepared to receive all that the Holy Spirit would do in our hearts we cannot accept the release of all that he would achieve through our lives.

3. Restore!
The Holy Spirit can then restore to our lives all those things which our human fears have refused to recognise. For God, the Father, by his Spirit has made us

joint-heirs with his Son and wants to give us gifts in order that we might fulfil his purposes here on planet earth.

An apocryphal story described a Christian arriving at the gates of heaven. He was warmly greeted by the archangel Gabriel who offered a personally guided tour around the vastness of heaven. The first building they visited was an enormous aircraft hanger lined with narrow shelves. Each shelf was filled with neatly wrapped presents all addressed to the new arrival.

'What's this, then? inquired the Christian.

'Oh, those,' replied Gabriel, 'they're all the gifts which God had for you to use on earth and which you never bothered to claim!'

Teaching – prophecy – service – giving – exhortation – hospitality – leadership – acts of kindness or mercy – word of knowledge – word of wisdom – faith – healing – miracles – discerning of spirits – tongues – interpretation of tongues – apostle – help – administration – exorcism – evangelism – pastorship – celibacy – voluntary martyrdom – mission – intercession and encouragement.

All those gifts are clearly recorded in Scripture. Some will come by natural means, others are supernaturally endowed. The more our lives are filled by the Spirit of God, the less we will demand to rule ourselves by human logic. When we bring to God our natural inclinations and abilities, asking him to bless what *we* have planned for *him* it is an invitation to spiritual disaster. Instead, our surrender to the direction of the Holy Spirit opens us to receive from him every gift which he wants to bestow on us.

There is a huge variety of gifts – and most of us are not limited to just one! In fact, if you can only identify one of these in your life then you must have it in abundance! These gifts are not for us to treasure and examine. They are given so that we can use them to bless and encourage others. 'Each one, as a good manager of God's different gifts, must use for the good of others the special gift he has received from God' (1 Pet. 4:10).

As C. Peter Wagner has so ably stated:

'Every spiritual gift we have is a resource which we must use and for which we will be held accountable at the judgement. Some will have one, some two, and some five. The quantity to begin with does not matter. Stewards are responsible only for what the master has chosen to give them. But the resource that we do have *must* be used to accomplish the master's purpose.'[2]

The gifts and talents which the Holy Spirit would restore to our lives are not meant to be used in isolation, but to complement those of other Christians whose gifts will be different from our own. We must be careful to recognise those gifts which God has given to us – and those which he has not. As J. B. Phillips has paraphrased Romans 12:3 'Try to have a sane estimate of your capabilities.' And do not be surprised when God gives you the opportunity to use gifts of which you are not even aware! He knows our potential far better than we do – after all, he made us! We must be prepared to experiment and discover from the positive response (or otherwise) of other Christians whether a particular gift is really of God or the produce of a fertile imagination.

If God has really given us a gift or talent, then results will inevitably follow. I was talking with a young evangelist who blurted out, 'I get so scared. I feel ill before preaching, I just don't know if evangelism is my gift or not.' I asked him what results he saw from his preaching. 'Oh, nearly always people are converted, often several come to real repentance.' I simply encouraged him to keep feeling scared! God was with him, because signs followed the use of his gift.

4. Reaffirm

It can be so easy for our love for Jesus to grow both stale and cold. At such times only the Holy Spirit can reveal Jesus, both to us and in us. We can know it as a fact that 'Our God Reigns'. But his sovereignty is demonstrated for us by the Holy Spirit, just so that we never forget!

Pam had been talking to her elderly neighbour for some time. Her neighbour knew of her connection with the fellowship and her Christian beliefs but Pam had held back from being too direct, feeling that she wanted to show the Christian life rather than preach it.

Pam met her neighbour near their local shop and had the usual chat about the weather as they went in. Pam felt the urge of the Spirit to talk of spiritual matters but didn't get round to it and her neighbour left the shop. Pam was regretting her reticence to share to gospel, but as she left the shop, she found her neighbour waiting. 'What I really wanted to talk to you about,' said the neighbour, 'was about Jesus and how you became a Christian!!'

Even in the middle of our failures, God wants to work it all out! At the back of all our fumbling attempts to do his will lies the all-powerful hand of the living God. He does not lie at a remote distance from us. For three years Jesus lived and moved with a small group of disciples. When they heard that he was leaving their hopes were shattered, their dreams broken in pieces. How dare he die and leave them alone?

Many Christians today have that same attitude.

They long to have walked by Galilee with Jesus, watched him heal the sick, feed the hungry and raise the dead, to have heard him speak his words of life. We forget that if Jesus still walked this earth in his physical form we might get to hear him once in our lifetime – but we'd have to live the rest of our lives on a memory.

Jesus told his disciples, '. . . it is better for you that I go away, because if I do not go, the Helper will not come to you' (John 16:7). To replace the memory we have the continuous presence of God, not just walking by us, but living in us.

With God in our lives, moving by his Spirit, amazing things can happen. A couple of years ago a great friend of mine, Mike Morris, was working as my assistant. We employed a secretary but, as Mike observed, a secretary is little use without a typewriter! Mike went straight ahead and ordered a typewriter. It had to match the other models which Youth for Christ possessed and the total cost was £600. There was no money available at all!

Mike felt absolutely convinced that it was within the will of God for this typewriter to be provided. Soon the machine arrived, so did the bill – but no money! We prayed and believed but nothing happened. Then, as the bill was due to be paid, Mike and I were driving up the M1 motorway late one night. We arrived at Rothersthorpe Service Station. I remember going into the 'Gents' while Mike filled the car with petrol. He picked me up on the way back from the station forecourt and we drove down the slipway back on to the motorway.

A few miles on Mike said, 'I was at the petrol pumps when I saw a ten pound note, then another, then another, then a whole bundle. I picked them up. I didn't hand them into the cashier, I thought we ought to take their directly to the Police. I think there's about six hundred pounds.' The Police searched for the owner of the money for three months with no success at all. At the end of that time Mike had the six hundred – and the typewriter . . .

I can't explain whether or not one of the Lord's people, or a church, was trying to hold out against the prompting of the Holy Spirit; or whether the Lord always intended the miracle. Either way there is tremendous security in knowing that we have a God who refuses to leave us to work out our own destinies. His interventions are the special demonstrations of his love and favour to us. It's just tremendous to know that 'Our God Reigns', and yet he cares for us and loves us in such a way that within the special boundaries of his will he provides our every need.

5. Release
The Holy Spirit longs to release the fragrance of God in our lives. We have emphasised his provision of gifts, but some people have said that the Christian life is not about gifts but fruit. In Galations 5:22 there is one fruit with nine flavours – love, joy, peace, patience, kindness, goodness, faithfulness, humility and self-control. They must always lie at the heart of the Christian life. But in no way do they constitute a threat or alternative to the operation of spiritual gifts.

Every major passage in the New Testament on the subject of gifts (1 Cor. 12, Rom. 12, Eph. 4, 1 Pet. 4) is accompanied by a passage on fruit. This is because fruit and gifts are not alternatives but co-essentials. The effective exercise of spiritual gifts depends upon the fruit of the Spirit. The Corinthian church tried to use one without the other and became a spiritual disaster area. As Peter Wagner says, 'Gifts without fruit are like a car tyre without air – the ingredients are all there, but they are worthless.'

There is a life-style which the Spirit of God would create among his people, no mere stereotype but the common characteristics lie in the fruit which he brings to birth among us. We will never be able to produce spiritual fruit by our own good resolutions or self-effort. It is a natural process, as fruit-bearing always is. After all, when did you last see an apple tree in the middle of an orchard struggling for breath, writhing in agony, and screaming to produce 'apples . . . pips . . . cores?' Yet many Christians seem to try to please God by this kind of process!

What does an apple tree require in order to grow and produce fruit? It needs sunlight, roots, moisture. Then growth becomes a natural process. In the same way if we are open to the sunlight of God's love, rooted in our relationship with him through the Bible and prayer, and also relaxing in the fulness of his Spirit, then growth and fruit are inevitable.

The problem for so many of us is that we are still trying too hard! We suffer from our vanity which demands that we must play a significant part in God's divine activities within our lives. Our insecurity shouts that all must follow the same spiritual pathway that we do. Our fears compel us to strive, and go on striving.

All our self-effort will never produce spiritual fruit, yet many of us excuse our lack of discipline in so many areas of our lives. We fail to recognise that our task is to renounce our sinful habits and ways, then Jesus can release his fruit within us by the gentle, natural, spontaneous operation of his Holy Spirit. We may not even notice the release but others won't fail to see the difference.

'Strive to get beyond mere pensive longing. Set your face like a flint and begin to put your life in order. Every man is as holy as he really wants to be. But the want must be all-compelling.

Tie up the loose ends of your life. Begin to tithe . . . institute family prayer . . . pay up your debts . . . make restitution . . . set aside time to pray and search the Scriptures . . . surrender wholly to the will of God.

Put away every un-Christian habit from you. If other Christians practise it without compunction, God may be calling you to come nearer to him than these care to come. Remember the words, "Others may, you cannot." Do not condemn or criticise, but seek a better way.

Get Christ himself in the focus of your heart and keep him there continually. Only in Christ will you find complete fulfilment.

Throw your heart open to the Holy Spirit and invite him to fill you. He will do it. Let no one interpret the Scriptures for you in such a way as to rule out the Father's gift of the Spirit. Every man is as full of the Spirit as he wants to be. Make your heart a vacuum and the Spirit will rush in to fill it.

Be hard on yourself and easy on others. Carry your own cross but never lay one on the back of another.

Begin to practise the presence of God.'

Then, when we come in loving simplicity, either alone, or with a friend to guide and help, God can and will release his Spirit within us. He will enable us to bear fruit, to witness to Jesus; he will give us strength to live and serve as God intended, and will lead us into a deeper and deeper love and worship of our Heavenly Father.

Two thousand years ago John the Baptist sent two

of his disciples to discover if Jesus was the Son of God. In reply Jesus used more than words. He healed the sick and blind and delivered the possessed. Then he replied, 'Go and tell John what you have seen and heard; the blind receive their sight, the lame walk, lepers are cleansed, and the deaf hear, the dead are raised up, the poor have good news preached to them' (Luke 7:22 RSV). Only the Holy Spirit can bear witness to Jesus and only he can make the dead live, the sick recover and the poor hear the gospel. But the amazing truth is that he, the living God, chooses to work through ordinary sinful men and women like you and me. He works to demonstrate the power and glory of Jesus, not just all those years ago in Palestine – but as it is today!

We are the hands and feet of Jesus; we must be available for him to use us. Not because *we* are in any way special but because he is the King of Kings and he longs to demonstrate that fact among us today. By his grace he deigns to stoop to our human frailty and work within us by his Spirit. How dare we make complaint when he chooses to work in a way other than our own? We must ask, as Moody did, that the Holy Spirit might do in our lives exactly what he wants to do; that by both miracles and acts of love Jesus may reveal himself. God alone knows what the result would be for our nation if an army of ordinary people was subject to the Spirit of God.

His activity is no mere attempt to show us new ways of enjoying ourselves. Paul reminds us that we are 'the body of Christ and individually members of it.' The Church must always live as a body and not retreat into the exclusiveness of a religious club. God has designed us to be participants in his purposes, not mere passengers. The experts say that, as individuals, people employ only about 30 per cent of their potential. So it has been in the body of Christ.

The Holy Spirit has always taken hold of, and used, simple, ordinary, and unlikely people. That is why Thomas, Peter, Mary Magdalene and a Samaritan woman were fit for his service. God takes us as we are, plain and ordinary, and therefore gets the glory himself. But we must stop looking at our weakness and face up to his strength.

When the Queen was a child, the story is told that she was playing at Balmoral with her sister. Inevitably they got lost and found themselves near a small house. The lady of the house had no idea who the two little girls were but offered them tea. She said to young Princess Elizabeth, 'Who are you, dear?' Back came the reply, 'Oh, I'm nobody, but my daddy's the King.'

We may be nobodies, the Church in Britain may be an insignificant speck on the horizon of society. But we worship and serve the King. In addition, we are his children – born and designed as containers for his Spirit.

We can face the future with hope, our society with courage, and ourselves with the knowledge that God can, and will, use even us. Because he *is* the King and we are his children. Because his spirit has come . . .

For many of us this truth is not enough. We stand on the wrong side of the Jordan, surveying the promised land, then turn sadly back to the sandy wastes of our old life-style. We regret the fears that prevent us going forward. But we are content with the Devil we know rather than the God who calls us on.

In the words of Graham Kendrick:

'If I don't follow you now
Perhaps I'll never know
All that you planned for me

The future that will never show . . .
Death is still the final truth
For all those friends I did not tell,
We believe that God loves everyone
Do we still believe in hell?
I wish I had that ancient fear of God
Which since has been mislaid,
I wish I had those eyes of simple trust
Like Jesus, when he prayed
So quiet and still,
To simply say it all,
Father I will.'

The making of a man or woman of God will always be in those simple words, belonging to a child in its Father's arms, simply looking up in confidence and trust to respond, 'Father, I will.'

PART THREE

THE EXAMPLE: WHY GOD USED D. L. MOODY

The 'why' of any life is always interesting, but when that life is an outstanding success it becomes doubly so. That Mr. Moody was a successful man no one would deny. He accomplished a lot during his lifetime and he left organisations on both sides of the Atlantic which are still triumphantly at work.

A contemporary of Moody said that he was a much more important evangelist than others because he was able to put new converts to work at once. Few men have had his ability to get others working. Indefatigable himself, he inspired others to go at it.

Moody was a Wesley, rather than a Whitefield, though he had many of the qualities of both. But like Wesley he did not depend on his preaching alone for results. He sought to leave something behind. Undoubtedly Whitefield was a better preacher than Wesley. He preached great sermons to huge throngs. He held 20,000 spellbound on Boston Common as he preached Christ, and many were saved. John Wesley perhaps faced smaller crowds, but he did not leave until he left the 'class meeting' behind. He left a little company and said to them, 'You go out and get others.' D. L. Moody believed that every Christian was to become a soul-winner.

Look around and see the institutions which Mr. Moody left in Great Britain and America. See his printed sermons still circulated by the scores of thousands yearly. See the steady line of young people going through the Bible Institute at Chicago to carry the gospel to the ends of the earth, and you will realise that Moody was a success.

God writes history in terms of human personality. The Book of Genesis gathers around eight men. The Bible presents epochs and eras, but at the centre of each is a personality, and generally the man is the key to the age.

Much of Old Testament history is summed up in the eleventh chapter of Hebrews, but it is presented as the story of human life. God's estimate of it all is seen in the men, Abel, Enoch, Noah, Abraham, Moses, and so on.

Is it too much to say that God is always looking for a man he can use? Notice the word 'use', for there seem to be four ideas concerning our relationship to God in service. Some teach that man is instructed of God. The divine command is given and man must obey. Others teach that in service man is helped of God. Still others, that he is led of God. All of these suggest a partnership with Deity. The fourth idea, and the right one, is that man can be used of God. This demands the surrender and submission of a Christian. This looks to God for enablement and gives to Him the glory.

Moody was used of God.

Men pass. Nations rise and fall. Customs change. Accepted philosophies are discarded like last year's garments. But it is ever true that God is looking for a man he can use. Will you be that man?

Will H. Houghton

On February 5, 1837, there was born of poor parents in a humble farmhouse in Northfield, Massachusetts, a little baby who was to become the greatest man, as I believe, of his generation or of his century – Dwight L. Moody.

After our great generals, great statesmen, great scientists and great men of letters have passed away and been forgotten, and their work and its helpful influence has come to an end, the work of D. L. Moody will go on and its saving influence continue and increase, bringing blessing not only to every state in the USA but to every nation on earth. Yes, it will continue throughout the ages of eternity.

I shall not seek to glorify Mr. Moody, but the God who by his grace, his entirely unmerited favor, used him so mightily, and the Christ who saved him by his atoning death and resurrection life, and the Holy Spirit who lived in him and wrought through him and who alone made him the mighty power that he was to this world.

Furthermore: I hope to make it clear that the God who used D. L. Moody in his day is just as ready to use you and me in this day if we, on our part, do what D. L. Moody did, which made it possible for God to so abundantly use him.

The whole secret of why D. L. Moody was such a mightily used man you will find in Psalm 62:11 (AV): 'God hath spoken once; twice have I heard this; that *power belongeth unto God*.' I am glad it does. I am glad that power did not belong to D. L. Moody; I am glad that it did not belong to Charles G. Finney; I am glad that it did not belong to Martin Luther; I am glad that it did not belong to any other Christian man whom God has greatly used in this world's history. Power belongs to God. If D. L. Moody had any power, and he had great power, he got it from God.

But God does not give his power arbitrarily. It is true that he gives it to whomsoever he will, but he wills to give it on certain conditions, which are clearly revealed in his Word. D. L. Moody met those conditions and God made him the most wonderful preacher of his generation; yes, I think the most wonderful man of his generation.

But how was it that D. L. Moody had that power of God so wonderfully manifested in his life? Pondering this question it seemed to me that there were seven things in the life of D. L. Moody that accounted for God's using him so largely as he did.

A Fully Surrendered Man

The first thing that accounts for God's using D. L. Moody so mightily was that *he was a fully surrendered man*. Every ounce of that two-hundred-and-eighty-pound body of his belonged to God. Everything he was and everything he had belonged wholly to God.

Now, I am not saying that Mr. Moody was perfect; he was not. If I attempted to, I presume I could point out some defects in his character. It does not occur to me at this moment what they were; but I am confident that I could think of some, if I tried hard enough.

I have never yet met a perfect man, not one. I have known perfect men in the sense in which the Bible commands us to be perfect; that is, men who are wholly God's, out-and-out for God, fully surrendered to God, with no will but God's will. But I have never known a man in whom I could not see some defects, some places where he might have been improved.

No, Mr. Moody was not a faultless man. If he had any flaws in his character, and he had, I presume I was in a position to know them better than almost any other man, because of my very close association with him in the later years of his life; and furthermore,

163

I suppose that in his latter days he opened his heart to me more fully than to anyone else in the world. I think he told me some things that he told no one else.

I presume I knew whatever defects there were in his character as well as anybody. But while I recognised such flaws, nevertheless, I know that he was a man who belonged wholly to God.

The first month I was in Chicago, we were having a talk about something upon which we very widely differed. Mr. Moody turned to me very frankly and very kindly and said in defence of his own position, 'Torrey, if I believed that God wanted me to jump out of that window, I would jump.' I believe he would. If he thought God wanted him to do anything he would do it. He belonged wholly, unreservedly, unqualifiedly, entirely, to God.

Henry Varley, a very intimate friend of Mr. Moody in the earlier days of his work, loved to tell how he once said to him, 'It remains to be seen what God will do with a man who gives himself up wholly to him.'

I am told that when Mr. Henry Varley said that, Mr. Moody said to himself, 'Well, I will be that man.'

And I, for my part, do not think 'it *remains* to be seen' what God will do with a man who gives himself up wholly to him. I think it has been seen already in D. L. Moody.

If you and I are to be used in our sphere as D. L. Moody was used in his, we must put all that we have and all that we are into the hands of God, for him to use as he will, to send us where he will, for God to do with us what he will, and we, on our part, to do everything God bids us do.

There are thousands and tens of thousands of men and women in Christian work, brilliant men and women, rarely gifted men and women, men and women who are making great sacrifices, men and women who have put all conscious sin out of their lives, yet who, nevertheless, have stopped short of absolute surrender to God, and therefore have stopped short of fulness of power.

But Mr. Moody did not stop short of absolute surrender to God; he was a wholly surrendered man, and if you and I are to be used, you and I must be wholly surrendered men and women.

A Man of Prayer

The second secret of the great power exhibited in Mr. Moody's life was that *Mr. Moody was in the deepest and most meaningful sense a man of prayer*. People often say to me, 'Well, I went many miles to see and to hear D. L. Moody and he certainly was a wonderful preacher.'

Yes, D. L. Moody certainly was a wonderful preacher; taking it all in all, the most wonderful preacher I have ever heard. It was a great privilege to hear him preach as he alone could preach; but out of a very intimate acquaintance with him I wish to testify that he was a far greater *pray-er* than he was preacher. Time and time again, he was confronted by obstacles that seemed insurmountable, but he always knew the way to surmount and to overcome all difficulties. He knew the way to bring to pass anything that needed to be brought to pass. He knew and believed in the deepest depths of his soul that 'nothing was too hard for the Lord' and that prayer could do anything that God could do.

Often Mr. Moody would write to me when he was about to undertake some new work, saying, 'I am beginning work in such and such a place on such and such a day; I wish you would get the students together for a day of fasting and prayer.' And often I have taken those letters and read them to the students in the lecture room and said, 'Mr. Moody wants us to have a day of fasting and prayer, first for God's blessing on our own souls and work, and then for God's blessing on him and his work.'

Often we were gathered in the lecture room far into the night – sometimes till one, two, three, four or even five o'clock in the morning, crying to God, just because Mr. Moody urged us to wait upon God until we received his blessing.

How many men and women I have known whose lives and characters have been transformed by those nights of prayer and who have wrought mighty things in many lands because of those nights of prayer!

One day Mr. Moody drove up to my house at Northfield and said, 'Torrey, I want you to take a ride with me.' I got into the carriage and we drove out toward Lover's Lane, talking about some great and unexpected difficulties that had arisen in regard to the work in Northfield and Chicago, and in connection with other work that was very dear to him.

As we drove along, some black storm-clouds lay ahead of us and then suddenly, as we were talking, it began to rain. He drove the horse into a shed near the entrance to Lover's Lane to shelter the horse, and then laid the reins upon the dashboard and said, 'Torrey, pray.' As best I could, I prayed, while he in his heart joined me in prayer. And when my voice was silent he began to pray. Oh, I wish you could have heard that prayer! I shall never forget it – so simple, so trustful, so definite, so direct, and so mighty.

When the storm was over and we drove back to town, the obstacles had been surmounted and the work of the schools, and other work that was threatened, went on as it had never gone on before, and it has gone on until this day.

As we drove back, Mr. Moody said to me. 'Torrey,

we will let the other men do the talking and the criticising, and we will stick to the work that God has given us to do, and let him take care of the difficulties and answer the criticisms.'

On one occasion Mr. Moody said to me in Chicago, 'I have just found, to my surprise, that we are twenty thousand dollars behind in our finances for the work here and in Northfield. We must have that twenty thousand dollars and I am going to get it by prayer.'

He did not tell a soul who had the ability to give a penny of the twenty thousand dollars deficit, but looked right to God and said, 'I need twenty thousand dollars for my work; send me that money in such a way that I will know it comes straight from Thee.' And God heard that prayer. The money came in such a way that it was clear that it came from God, in direct answer to prayer.

Yes, D. L. Moody was a man who believed in the God who answers prayer, and not only believed in him in a theoretical way but believed in him in a practical way. He was a man who met every difficulty that stood in his way – by prayer. Everything he undertook was backed up by prayer, and in everything, his ultimate dependence was upon God.

A Deep and Practical Student of the Bible

The third secret of Mr. Moody's power, or the third reason why God used D. L. Moody, was because *he was a deep and practical student of the Word of God*.

It is often said of D. L. Moody that he was not a student. I wish to say that he *was* a student; most emphatically he was a student. He was not a student of psychology; he was not a student of anthropology – I am very sure he would not have known what that word meant; he was not a student of biology; he was not a student of philosophy; he was not even a student of theology, in the technical sense of the term; but he was a student, a profound and practical student of the one book that is more worth studying than all other books in the world put together; he was a student of the Bible.

Every day of his life, I have reason for believing, he arose very early in the morning to study the Word of God, way down to the close of his life. Mr. Moody used to rise about four o'clock in the morning to study the Bible. He would say to me: 'If I am going to get in any study, I have got to get up before the other folks get up,' and he would shut himself up in a remote room in his house, alone with his God and his Bible.

I shall never forget the first night I spent in his home. He had invited me to take the superintendency of the Bible Institute and I had already begun my work. I was on my way to some city in the East to preside at the International Christian Workers' Convention. He wrote me saying, 'Just as soon as the Convention is over, come up to Northfield.'

He learned when I was likely to arrive and drove over to South Vernon to meet me. That night he had all the teachers from the Mount Hermon School and from the Northfield Seminary come together at the house to meet me, and to talk over the problems of the two schools.

We talked together far on into the night, and then, after the principals and teachers of the schools had gone home, Mr. Moody and I talked together about the problems a while longer. It was very late when I got to bed that night, but very early the next morning, about five o'clock, I heard a gentle tap on my door. Then I heard Mr. Moody's voice whispering, 'Torrey, are you up?' I happened to be; I do not always get up at that early hour but I happened to be up that particular morning. He said, 'I want you to go somewhere with me', and I went down with him. Then I found out that he had already been up an hour or two in his room studying the Word of God.

Oh, you may talk about power; but, if you neglect the one book that God has given you as the one instrument through which he imparts and exercises his power, you will not have it. You may read many books and go to many conventions and you may have your all-night prayer meetings to pray for the power of the Holy Ghost; but unless you keep in constant and close association with the one book, the Bible, you will not have power. And if you ever had power, you will not maintain it except by the daily, earnest, intense study of that book. *Ninety-nine Christians in every hundred are merely playing at Bible-study; and therefore ninety-nine Christians in every hundred are mere weaklings, when they might be giants, both in their Christian life and in their service.*

It was largely because of his thorough knowledge of the Bible, and his practical knowledge of the Bible, that Mr. Moody drew such immense crowds. On 'Chicago Day', in October, 1893, none of the theatres of Chicago dared to open because it was expected that everybody in Chicago would go on that day to the World's Fair; and, in point of fact, something like four hundred thousand people did pass through the gates of the Fair that day.

Everybody in Chicago was expected to be at that end of the city on that day. But Mr. Moody said to me, 'Torrey, engage the Central Music Hall and announce meetings from nine o'clock in the morning till six o'clock at night.'

'Why,' I replied, 'Mr. Moody, nobody will be at this end of Chicago on that day; not even the theatres dare to open; everybody is going down to Jackson

Park to the Fair; we cannot get anybody out on this day.'

Mr. Moody replied, 'You do as you are told,' and I did as I was told and engaged the Central Music Hall for continuous meetings from nine o'clock in the morning till six o'clock at night. But I did it with a heavy heart; I thought there would be poor audiences.

I was on the programme at noon that day. Being very busy in my office about the details of the campaign, I did not reach the Central Music Hall until almost noon. I thought I would have no trouble in getting in. But when I got almost to the hall I found to my amazement that not only was it packed but the vestibule was packed and the steps were packed, and there was no getting anywhere near the door. If I had not gone around and climbed in a back window they would have lost their speaker for that hour. But that would not have been of much importance, for the crowds had not gathered to hear me, it was the magic of Mr. Moody's name that had drawn them. And why did they long to hear Mr. Moody? Because they knew that while he was not versed in many of the philosophies and fads and fancies of the day, he did know the one book that this old world most longs to know – the Bible.

I shall never forget Moody's last visit to Chicago. The ministers of Chicago had sent me to Cincinnati to invite him to come to Chicago and hold a meeting. In response to the invitation, Mr. Moody said to me, 'If you will hire the Auditorium for weekday mornings and afternoons, and have meetings at ten in the morning and three in the afternoon, I will go.''

I replied, 'Mr. Moody, you know what a busy city Chicago is, and how impossible it is for businessmen to get out at ten o'clock in the morning and three in the afternoon on working days. Will you not hold evening meetings and meetings on Sunday?'

'No,' he replied, 'I am afraid if I did, I would interfere with the regular work of the churches.'

I went back to Chicago and engaged the Auditorium, which at that time was the building having the largest seating capacity of any building in the city, seating in those days about seven thousand people. I announced weekday meetings, with Mr. Moody as the speaker, at ten o'clock in the mornings and three o'clock in the afternoons.

At once protests began to pour in upon me. One of them came from Marshall Field, at that time the business king of Chicago. 'Mr. Torrey,' Mr. Field wrote, 'we businessmen of Chicago wish to hear Mr. Moody, and you know perfectly well how impossible it is for us to get out at ten o'clock in the morning and three o'clock in the afternoon. Have evening meetings.'

I received many letters of a similar purport and wrote to Mr. Moody urging him to give us evening meetings. But Mr. Moody simply replied, 'You do as you are told,' and I did as I was told. That is the way I kept my job.

On the first morning of the meetings I went down to the Auditorium about half an hour before the appointed time, but I went with much fear and apprehension. I thought the Auditorium would be nowhere nearly full. When I reached there, to my amazement, I found a queue of people, four abreast, extending from the Congress Street entrance to Wabash Avenue, then a block north on Wabash Avenue, then a break to let traffic through, and then another block, and so on. I went in through the back door, and there were many clamouring for entrance there.

When the doors were opened at the appointed time, we had a cordon of twenty policemen to keep back the crowd; but the crowd was so great that it swept the cordon of policemen off their feet and packed eight thousand people into the building before we could get the doors shut. And I think there were as many left on the outside as there were in the building. I do not think that anyone else in the world could have drawn such a crowd at such a time.

Why? Because though Mr. Moody knew little about science, or philosophy, or literature in general, he did know the one book that this old world is perishing to know and longing to know. And this old world will flock to hear men who know the Bible and preach the Bible as they will flock to hear nothing else on earth.

During all the months of the World's Fair in Chicago, no one could draw such crowds as Mr. Moody. Judging by the papers, one would have thought that the great religious event in Chicago at that time was the World's Congress of Religions. One very gifted man of letters in the East was invited to speak at this Congress. He saw in this invitation the opportunity of his life and prepared his paper, the exact title of which I do not now recall, but it was something along the line of: 'New Light on the Old Doctrines.'

He prepared the paper with great care, and then sent it around to his most trusted and gifted friends for criticisms. These men sent it back to him with such emendations as they had to suggest. Then he rewrote the paper, incorporating as many of the suggestions and criticisms as seemed wise. Then he sent it around for further criticisms. Then he wrote the paper a third time, and had it, as he trusted, perfect.

He went on to Chicago to meet this coveted opportunity of speaking at the World's Congress of Religions. It was at eleven o'clock on a Saturday morning (if I remember correctly) that he was to speak. He stood outside the door of the platform waiting for the great moment to arrive, and as the clock struck eleven walked on to the platform to face a magnificent audience of eleven women and two men! But there was not a building anywhere in Chicago that would accommodate, the very same day, the crowds that would flock to hear Mr. Moody at any hour of the day or night.

If you wish to get an audience and wish to do that audience some good after you get them, *study*, study, STUDY the one book, and *preach*, preach, PREACH the one book, and *teach*, teach, TEACH the one book, the Bible, the only book that contains God's Word, and the only book that has power to gather and hold and bless the crowds for any great length of time.

A Humble Man

The fourth reason why God continuously, through so many years, used D. L. Moody was because *he was a humble man*. I think D. L. Moody was the humblest man I ever knew in all my life. He loved to quote the words of another: 'Faith gets the most; love works the most; but *humility keeps the most*.' He himself had the humility that keeps everything it gets.

As I have already said, he was the most humble man I ever knew, that is, the most humble man when we bear in mind the great things he did, and the praise that was lavished upon him. Oh, how he loved to put himself in the background and put other men in the foreground! How often he would stand on a platform with some of us little fellows seated behind him and as he spoke he would say, 'There are better men coming after me.' As he said it, he would point back over his shoulder with his thumb to the 'little fellows.' I do not know how he could believe it, but he really *did* believe that the others that were coming after him were really better than he was.

He made no pretence to a humility he did not possess. In his heart of hearts he constantly underestimated himself, and overestimated others. He really believed that God would use other men in a larger measure than he had been used.

Mr. Moody loved to keep himself in the background. At his conventions at Northfield, or anywhere else, he would push the other men to the front and, if he could, have them do all the preaching – McGregor, Campbell Morgan, Andrew Murray, and the rest of them.

The only way we could get him to take any part in the programme was to get up in the convention and move that we hear D. L. Moody at the next meeting. He continually put himself out of sight.

Oh, how many a man has been full of promise and God has used him, and then the man thought that he was the whole thing and God was compelled to set him aside! I believe more promising workers have gone on the rocks through self-sufficiency and self-esteem than through any other cause.

I can look back for forty years, or more, and think of many men who are now wrecks or derelicts who at one time the world thought were going to be something great. But they have disappeared entirely from the public view. Why? Because of overestimation of self.

I remember a man with whom I was closely associated in a great movement in this country. We were having a most successful convention in Buffalo, and he was greatly elated. As we walked down the street together to one of the meetings one day, he said to me, 'Torrey, you and I are the most important men in Christian work in this country,' or words to that effect.

I replied, 'John, I am sorry to hear you say that; for as I read my Bible I find man after man who had accomplished great things whom God had to set aside because of his sense of his own importance.' And God set that man aside also from that time. I think he is still living, but no one ever hears of him, or has heard of him for years.

God used D. L. Moody, I think, beyond any man of his day; but it made no difference how much God used him, he never was puffed up.

One day, speaking to me of a great New York preacher, now dead, Mr. Moody said, 'He once did a very foolish thing, the most foolish thing that I ever knew a man, ordinarily so wise as he was, to do. He came up to me at the close of a little talk I had given and said, "Young man, you have made a great address tonight." ' Then Mr. Moody continued, 'How foolish of him to have said that! It almost turned my head.'

But, thank God it did *not* turn his head, and even when nearly all the ministers in England, Scotland and Ireland, and many of the English bishops were ready to follow D. L. Moody wherever he led, even then it never turned his head one bit. He would get down on his face before God, knowing he was human, and ask God to empty him of all self-sufficiency. And God did.

Men and women – especially young men and young women – perhaps God is beginning to use you! Very likely people are saying, 'What a wonderful gift he has as a Bible teacher. What power he has as a preacher, for such a young man!'

Listen – get down upon your face before God. I believe here lies one of the most dangerous snares of the Devil. When the Devil cannot discourage a man, he approaches him on another tack, which he knows is far worse in its results – he puffs him up by whispering in his ear, 'You are the leading evangelist of the day. You are the man who will sweep everything before you. You are the coming man. You are the D. L. Moody of the day,' and if you listen to him, he will ruin you.

The entire shore of the history of Christian workers is strewn with the wrecks of gallant vessels that were full of promise a few years ago, but these men became puffed up and were driven on the rocks by the wild winds of their own raging self-esteem.

His Entire Freedom from the Love of Money

The fifth secret of D. L. Moody's continual power and usefulness was *his entire freedom from the love of money*. Mr. Moody might have been a wealthy man, but money had no charms for him. He loved to gather money for God's work; he refused to accumulate money for himself.

He told me during the World's Fair that if he had taken for himself the royalties on the hymn books which he had published, they would have amounted, at that time, to a million dollars. But Mr. Moody refused to touch the money. He had a perfect right to take it, for he was responsible for the publication of the books and it was his money that went into the publication of the first of them.

Mr. Sankey had some hymns that he had taken with him to England and he wished to have them published. He went to a publisher who declined to publish them because, as was said, Philip Phillips had recently been over and published a hymn book and it had not done well. However, Mr. Moody had a little money and he said that he would put it into the publication of these hymns in cheap form, and he did.

The hymns had a most remarkable and unexpected sale. They were then published in book form and large profits accrued. The financial results were offered to Mr. Moody, but he refused to touch them. 'But,' it was urged on him, 'the money belongs to you.' But he would not touch it.

Mr. Fleming H. Revell was at the time treasurer of the Chicago Avenue Church, commonly known as the Moody Tabernacle. Only the basement of this new church building had been completed, funds having been exhausted. Hearing of the hymn book situation Mr. Revell suggested, in a letter to friends in London, that the money be given for completion of this building, and it was.

Afterwards, so much money came in that it was given, by the committe into whose hands Mr. Moody put the matter, to various Christian enterprises.

In a certain city to which Mr. Moody went in the latter years of his life, and where I went with him, it was publicly announced that Mr. Moody would accept no money whatever for his services. Now, in point of fact, Mr. Moody was dependent, in a measure, upon what was given him at various services; but when this announcement was made Mr. Moody said nothing, and left that city without a penny's compensation for the hard work he did there; and, I think, he paid his own hotel bill.

And yet a minister in that very city came out with an article in a paper, which I read, in which he told a fairy tale of the financial demands that Mr. Moody made upon them, which story I knew personally to be absolutely untrue.

Millions of dollars passed into Mr. Moody's hands, *but they passed through*; they did not stick to *his* fingers.

This is the point at which many an evangelist makes shipwreck, and his great work comes to an untimely end. The love of money on the part of some evangelists has done more to discredit evangelistic work in our day, and to lay many an evangelist on the shelf, than almost any other cause.

While I was away on a tour I was told by one of the most reliable ministers in one of our eastern cities of a campaign conducted by one who had been greatly used in the past.

This evangelist came to a city for a united evangelistic campaign and was supported by fifty-three churches. The minister who told me about the matter was himself chairman of the Finance Committee. The evangelist showed such a longing for money and so deliberately violated the agreement he had made before coming to the city and so insisted upon money being gathered for him in other ways than he had himself prescribed in the original contract, that this minister threatened to resign from the Finance Committee. He was, however, persuaded to remain to avoid a scandal.

'As the total result of the three weeks' campaign there were only twenty-four clear decisions,' said my friend, 'and after it was over the ministers got together and by a vote, with but one dissenting voice, they agreed to send a letter to this evangelist telling him frankly that they were done with him and with his methods of evangelism for ever, and that they felt it their duty to warn other cities against him and his methods and the results of his work.'

Let us lay the lesson to our hearts and take warning in time.

His Consuming Passion for the Salvation of the Lost

The sixth reason why God used D. L. Moody was because of *his consuming passion for the salvation of the lost*. Mr. Moody made the resolution, shortly after he himself was saved, that he would never let twenty-four hours pass over his head without speaking to at least one person about his soul.

His was a very busy life, and sometimes he would forget his resolution until the last hour, and sometimes he would get out of bed, dress, go out and talk to someone about his soul in order that he might not let one day pass without having definitely told at least one of his fellow-mortals about his need and the Saviour who could meet it.

One night Mr. Moody was going home from his place of business. It was very late, and it suddenly occurred to him that he had not spoken to one single person that day about accepting Christ. He said to himself, 'Here's a day lost. I have not spoken to anyone today and I shall not see anybody at this late hour.'

But as he walked up the street he saw a man standing under a lamp-post. The man was a perfect stranger to him, though it turned out afterwards the man knew who Mr. Moody was. He stepped up to this stranger and said, 'Are you a Christian?'

The man replied, 'That is none of your business, whether I am a Christian or not. If you were not a sort of a preacher I would knock you into the gutter for your impertinence.'

Mr. Moody said a few earnest words and passed on. The next day that man called upon one of Mr. Moody's prominent business friends and said to him, 'That man Moody of yours over on the North Side is doing more harm than he is good. He has got zeal without knowledge. He stepped up to me last night, a perfect stranger, and insulted me. He asked me if I were a Christian, and I told him it was none of his business and if he were not a sort of a preacher I would knock him into the gutter for his impertinence. He is doing more harm than he is good. He has got . zeal without knowledge.'

Mr. Moody's friend sent for him and said, 'Moody, you are doing more harm than you are good; you've got zeal without knowledge: you insulted a friend of mine on the street last night. You went up to him, a perfect stranger, and asked him if he were a Christian, and he tells me if you had not been a sort of a preacher he would have knocked you into the gutter for your impertinence. You are doing more harm than you are good; you have got zeal without knowledge.'

Mr. Moody went out of that man's office somewhat crestfallen. He wondered if he were not doing more harm than he was good, if he really had zeal without knowledge. (Let me say, in passing, it is far better to have zeal without knowledge than it is to have knowledge without zeal. Some men and women are as full of knowledge as an egg is of meat. They are so deeply versed in Bible truth that they can sit in criticism on the preachers and give the preachers pointers, but they have so little zeal that they do not lead one soul to Christ in a whole year.)

Weeks passed by. One night Mr. Moody was in bed when he heard a tremendous pounding at his front door. He jumped out of bed and rushed to the door. He thought the house was on fire. He thought the man would break down the door. He opened the door and there stood this man. He said, 'Mr. Moody, I have not had a good night's sleep since that night you spoke to me under the lamp-post, and I have come around at this unearthly hour of the night for you to tell me what I have to do to be saved.'

Mr. Moody took him in and told him what to do to be saved. Then he accepted Christ, and when the

Civil War broke out he went to the front and laid down his life fighting for his country.

Another night, Mr. Moody got home and had gone to bed before it occurred to him that he had not spoken to a soul that day about accepting Christ. 'Well,' he said to himself, 'it is no good getting up now; there will be nobody on the street at this hour of the night.' But he got up, dressed and went to the front door.

It was pouring with rain. 'Oh,' he said, 'there will be no one out in this pouring rain.' Just then he heard the patter of a man's feet as he came down the street, holding an umbrella over his head. Then Mr. Moody darted out and rushed up to the man and said, 'May I share the shelter of your umbrella?' 'Certainly,' the man replied. Then Mr. Moody said, 'Have you any shelter in the time of storm?' and preached Jesus to him.

If only we were as full of zeal for the salvation of souls as that, how long would it be before the whole country would be shaken by the power of a mighty, God-sent revival?

One day in Chicago – the day after the elder Carter Harrison was shot, when his body was lying in state in the City Hall – Mr. Moody and I were riding up Randolph Street together in a streetcar right alongside the City Hall. The car could scarcely get through because of the enormous crowds waiting to get in and view the body of Mayor Harrison.

As the car tried to push its way through the crowd, Mr. Moody turned to me and said, 'Torrey, what does this mean?' 'Why,' I said, 'Carter Harrison's body lies there in the City Hall and these crowds are waiting to see it.'

Then he said, 'This will never do, to let these crowds get away from us without preaching to them;

we must talk to them. You go and hire Hooley's Opera House (which was just opposite the City Hall) for the whole day.' I did so. The meetings began at nine o'clock in the morning, and we had one continuous service from that hour until six in the evening, to reach those crowds.

Mr. Moody was a man on fire for God. Not only was he always 'on the job' himself but he was always getting others to work as well.

He once invited me down to Northfield to spend a month there with the school, speaking first to one school and then crossing the river to the other. I was obliged to use the ferry a great deal. It was before the present bridge was built at that point.

One day he said to me, 'Torrey, did you know that that ferryman that ferries you across every day was unconverted?' He did not tell me to speak to him, but I knew what he meant. When some days later it was told him that the ferryman was saved, he was exceedingly happy.

Once, when walking down a certain street in Chicago, Mr. Moody stepped up to a man, a perfect stranger to him, and said, 'Sir, are you a Christian?'

'You, mind your own business,' was the reply.

Mr. Moody replied: 'This is my business.'

The man said, 'Well, then, you must be Moody.'

Out in Chicago they used to call him in those early days, 'Crazy Moody', because day and night he was speaking to everybody he got a chance to speak to about being saved.

One time he was going to Milwaukee, and in the seat that he had chosen sat a travelling man. Mr. Moody sat down beside him and immediately began to talk with him. 'Where are you going?' Mr. Moody asked. When told the name of the town he said, 'We will soon be there, we'll have to get down to business at once. Are you saved?' The man said that he was not, and Mr. Moody took out his Bible and there on the train showed him the way of salvation. Then he said, 'Now, you must take Christ.' The man did; he was converted right there on the train.

Most of you have heard, I presume, the story President Wilson used to tell about D. L. Moody. Ex-President Wilson said that he once went into a barber shop and took a chair next to the one in which D. L. Moody was sitting, though he did not know that Mr. Moody was there. He had not been in the chair very long before, as ex-President Wilson phrased it, he 'knew there was a personality in the other chair,' and he began to listen to the conversation going on. He heard Mr. Moody tell the barber about the Way of Life, and President Wilson said, 'I have never forgotten that scene to this day.' When Mr. Moody was gone, he asked the barber who he was. When he was told that it was D. L. Moody, President Wilson said, 'It made an impression upon me I have not yet forgotten.'

On one occasion in Chicago Mr. Moody saw a little girl standing on the street with a pail in her hand. He went up to her and invited her to his Sunday school, telling her what a pleasant place it was. She promised to go the following Sunday, but she did not do so.

Mr. Moody watched for her for weeks, and then one day he saw her on the street again, at some distance from him. He started toward her, but she saw him too and started to run away. Mr. Moody followed her. Down one street she went, Mr. Moody after her; up another street she went, Mr. Moody after her; through an alley, Mr. Moody still following; out on another street, Mr. Moody after her; then she dashed into a saloon and Mr. Moody dashed after her. She ran out of the back door and up a flight of stairs, Mr.

Moody still following. She dashed into a room, Mr. Moody following. She threw herself under the bed and Mr. Moody reached under the bed and pulled her out by the foot, and led her to Christ.

He found that her mother was a widow who had once seen better circumstances, but had gone down until she was living over this saloon. She had several children. Mr. Moody led the mother and all the family to Christ. Several of the children were prominent members of the Moody Church until they moved away, and afterwards became prominent in churches elsewhere.

This particular child, whom he pulled from underneath the bed, was, when I was the pastor of the Moody Church, the wife of one of the most prominent officers in the church.

Only two or three years ago, as I came out of a ticket office in Memphis, Tennessee, a fine-looking young man followed me. He said, 'Are you not Dr. Torrey?' I said, 'Yes.' He said, 'I am so and so.' He was the son of this woman. He was then a travelling man and an officer in the church where he lived.

When Mr. Moody pulled that little child out from under the bed by the foot he was pulling a whole family into the Kingdom of God, and eternity alone will reveal how many succeeding generations he was pulling into the Kingdom of God.

D. L. Moody's consuming passion for souls was not for the souls of those who would be helpful to him in building up his work here or elsewhere. His love for souls knew no class limitation. He was no respecter of persons; it might be an earl or a duke or it might be an ignorant coloured boy on the street; it was all the same to him. There was a soul to save and he did what lay in his power to save that soul.

A friend once told me that the first time he ever

heard of Mr. Moody was when Mr. Reynolds of Peoria told him that he once found Mr. Moody sitting in one of the squatters' shanties that used to be in that part of the city towards the lake, which was then called, 'The Sands,' with a coloured boy on his knee, a tallow candle in one hand and a Bible in the other. Mr. Moody was spelling out the words (for at that time the boy could not read very well) of certain verses of Scripture, in an attempt to lead that ignorant coloured boy to Christ.

If you and I were on fire for souls like that, how long would it be before we had a revival? Pray that tonight the fire of God falls and fills our hearts – a burning fire that will send us out all over the country, and across the water to China, Japan, India, and Africa, to tell lost souls the way of salvation!

Definitely Endued with Power from on High

The seventh thing that was the secret of why God used D. L. Moody was that *he had a very definite enduement with power from on high, a very clear and definite baptism with the Holy Ghost*. Mr. Moody knew he had "the baptism with the Holy Ghost"; he had no doubt about it.

In his early days he was a great hustler; he had a tremendous desire to do something, but he had no real power. He worked very largely in the energy of the flesh. But there were two humble Free Methodist women who used to come over to his meetings in the YMCA. One was 'Auntie Cook' and the other Mrs. Snow.

These two women would come to Mr. Moody at the close of his meetings and say, 'We are praying for you.'

Finally, Mr. Moody became somewhat nettled and

said to them one night, 'Why are you praying for me? Why don't you pray for the unsaved?'

They replied, 'We are praying that you may get the power.'

Mr. Moody did not know what that meant, but he got to thinking about it, and then went to these women and said, 'I wish you would tell me what you mean'. So they told him about the definite baptism with the Holy Ghost. Then he asked that he might pray with them and not that they merely pray for him.

Auntie Cook once told me of the intense fervour with which Mr. Moody prayed on that occasion. She told me in words that I scarcely dare repeat, though I have never forgotten them. And he not only prayed with them, but he also prayed alone.

Not long after he was walking up Wall Street in New York; (Mr. Moody very seldom told this and I almost hesitate to tell it) and in the midst of the bustle and hurry of that city his prayer was answered. The power of God fell upon him as he walked up the street and he had to hurry off to the house of a friend and ask that he might have a room by himself. In that room he stayed alone for hours; and the Holy Ghost came upon him filling his soul with such joy that at last he had to ask God to withhold his hand, lest he die on the spot from very joy.

He went out from that place with the power of the Holy Ghost upon him. When he later got to London (partly through the prayers of a bedridden saint in Mr. Lessey's church), the power of God wrought through him mightily in North London, and hundreds were added to the churches. That was what led to his being invited over to the wonderful campaign that followed in later years.

Time and again Mr. Moody would come to me and

say, 'Torrey, I want you to preach on baptism with the Holy Ghost.' I do not know how many times he asked me to speak on that subject.

Once, when I had been invited to preach in the Fifth Avenue Presbyterian Church, New York, (invited at Mr. Moody's suggestion; had it not been for his suggestion the invitation would never have been extended to me), just before I started for New York, Mr. Moody drove up to my house and said, 'Torrey, they want you to preach at the Fifth Avenue Presbyterian Church in New York. It is a great, big church, cost a million dollars to build it.' Then he continued, 'Torrey, I just want to ask one thing of you. I want to tell you what to preach about. You will preach that sermon of yours on 'Ten reasons why I believe the Bible to be the Word of God' and your sermon on 'The baptism with the Holy Ghost.''

Time and again, when a call came to me to go off to some church, he would come up to me and say, 'Now, Torrey, be sure and preach on the baptism with the Holy Ghost.' I do not know how many times he said that to me.

Once I asked him, 'Mr. Moody, don't you think I have any sermons but those two?'

'Never mind that,' he replied, 'you give them those two sermons.'

Once he had some teachers at Northfield – fine men, all of them, but they did not believe in a definite baptism with the Holy Ghost for the individual. They believed that every child of God was baptized with the Holy Ghost, and they did not believe in any special baptism with the Holy Ghost for the individual.

Mr. Moody came to me and said, 'Torrey, will you come up to my house after the meeting tonight and I will get those men to come, and I want you to talk this thing out with them.'

Of course, I very readily consented, and Mr. Moody and I talked for a long time, but they did not altogether see eye to eye with us. And when they went, Mr. Moody signalled me to remain for a few moments. Mr. Moody sat there with his chin on his breast, as he so often sat when he was in deep thought; then he looked up and said, 'Oh, why will they split hairs? Why don't they see that this is just the one thing that they themselves need? They are good teachers, they are wonderful teachers, and I am so glad to have them here; but why will they not see that the baptism with the Holy Ghost is just the one touch that they themselves need?'

I shall never forget July 8, 1894, to my dying day. It was the closing day of the Northfield Students' Conference – the gathering of the students from the eastern colleges. Mr. Moody had asked me to preach on Saturday night and Sunday morning on the baptism with the Holy Ghost.

On Saturday night I had spoken about, 'The Baptism with the Holy Ghost: What It Is; What It Does; The Need of It and the Possibility of It.' On Sunday morning I spoke on 'The Baptism with the Holy Spirit: How to Get It.' It was just exactly twelve o'clock when I finished my morning sermon, and I took out my watch and said, 'Mr. Moody has invited us all to go up on the mountain at three o'clock this afternoon to pray for the power of the Holy Spirit. It is three hours to three o'clock. Some of you cannot wait three hours. You do not need to wait. Go to your rooms; go out into the woods; go to your tent; go anywhere where you can get alone with God and have this matter out with him.'

At three o'clock we all gathered in front of Mr. Moody's mother's house (she was then still living), and then began to pass down the lane, through the gate, up on to the mountainside. There were four hundred and fifty-six of us in all; I know the number because Paul Moody counted us as we passed through the gate.

After awhile Mr. Moody said, 'I don't think we need to go any further; let us sit down here.' We sat down on stumps and logs and on the ground. Mr. Moody said, 'Have any of you students anything to say?'

I think about seventy-five of them arose, one after the other, and said, 'Mr. Moody, I could not wait till three o'clock; I have been alone with God since the morning service, and I believe I have a right to say that I have been baptized with the Holy Spirit.'

When these testimonies were over, Mr. Moody said, 'Young men, I can't see any reason why we shouldn't kneel down here right now and ask God that the Holy Ghost may fall upon us just as definitely as he fell upon the apostles on the Day of Pentecost. Let us pray.' And we did pray, there on the mountainside.

As we had gone up the mountainside heavy clouds had been gathering, and just as we began to pray those clouds broke and the raindrops began to fall through the overhanging pines. But there was another cloud that had been gathering over Northfield for ten days, a cloud big with the mercy and grace and power of God; and as we began to pray our prayers seemed to pierce that cloud and the Holy Ghost fell upon us.

Men and women, that is what we all need – the baptism with the Holy Ghost.

NOTES
PART TWO

Chapter 1
1. Leighton Ford, *The Christian Persuader*
2. A. W. Tozer, *The Divine Conquest*
3. Malcolm Muggeridge, *Another King*

Chapter 4
1. H. B. Dehqani-Tafti, *The Hard Awakening* (Triangle 1981)
2. Leighton Ford, *One Way to Change the World*
3. Samuel Escober, *The Social Responsibility of the Church* (Latin American Congress on Evangelism, Bogota 1969)
4. Jim Wallis, *Agenda for Biblical People* (Harper & Row 1976)

Chapter 5
1. The Jam – *Sound Affects – From the Cradle to the Grave* (Weller 1980 Polydor)
2. John White, *The Golden Cow* (Lakeland 1979)
3. William Barclay, *The Epistles of James*
4. Clifford Hill, *Toward the Dawn* (Collins 1980)
5. David C K Watson, *I Believe in the Church*, Hodders & Stoughton 1978
6. Eric Delve, *To Boldly Go* (Marshalls 1979)
7. Stewardship Development Dept., Episcopal Church of America. From Malcolm Widdecombe, Renewal Magazine (June/July 1982)

Chapter 6
1. Rebecca Manley Pippert, *Out of the Saltshaker* (IVP 1979)
2. A. W. Tozer, *Paths to Power*
3. Henry Drummond, *The Greatest Thing in the World*

Chapter 7
1. A. W. Tozer,
2. C. Peter Wagner,

Other Marshalls Books

WITH A CHURCH LIKE THIS WHO NEEDS SATAN?

Clive Calver

Beware—Satan is at large in the Church of Britain today and he is using you to do his work for him!

Clive Calver declares it is time to stand aside and look to God to restore our sense of urgency and compassion, to give us a new vision and a new hope. It is time to regain faith in ourselves, in those around us, and in the God who is waiting to achieve through us all that he has promised. To fulfil our true potential as sons of God and heirs to heaven.

THE PRACTICE OF BIBLICAL MEDITATION

Campbell McAlpine

Did you know that the Bible recommends meditation?

Meditation can bring you peace of mind and strengthen your faith. It is a divinely approved way of coming closer to God. But there is a right way and a wrong way. This book gives you the lessons which the Bible writers learnt and the methods they recommend. It gives you day to day instructions on how you can meditate and find inner security. It measures the results you can obtain.

Biblical meditation will transform your life. Learn it, practice it, preach it.

KINGDOM HEALING

Trevor Martin

Why does so much of the Gospel narrative consist of healing miracles? How did the original—and tiny—company of believers 'turn the world upside down'?

For centuries, claims Trevor Martin, the Church has neglected the second half of its timeless commission to 'preach the Gospel and heal the sick'. He shows how both in the ministry of Jesus and the Apostolic Church, preaching and healing were inseparable—and God still wants them to be so! His love for the whole being of Man has not diminished, nor has his power.

God did not only heal supernaturally in Bible days, he wants to heal in the same way today. He can, and still does, act in power.

RADICAL DISCIPLESHIP

Chris Sugden

Christ is living amongst us. Not in the churches of the English middle-class but in the slums of Bombay, the horrors of Cambodia, the savage feudal wars of Central America. He is the same today as he was 2 000 years ago, when he made friends with the outcasts, the lepers, the prostitutes, the tax-collectors, and condemned the Pharisees for their hardness of heart.

We crucify him every day we do not protest against the evil which allows two thirds of the world's population to starve, which allows oppression, injustice, racial and class prejudice to rage unchecked, every day in which we do not alleviate their suffering and pray that our indifference might be forgiven.

We can only truly experience the liberating freedom which the cross brought if we surrender to the demands Christ makes of us. Isn't it about time we stepped down from our pedestals, got our hands dirty and took the whole gospel seriously?